I0832811

FIVE YEARS

IN

THE ALLEGHANIES.

PUBLISHED BY THE
AMERICAN TRACT SOCIETY,
150 NASSAU-STREET, NEW YORK.

BV
3785
.C81
A3
1863

Buhr

Entered according to Act of Congress, in the year 1863, by the AMERICAN TRACT SOCIETY, in the Clerk's Office of the District Court of the Southern District of the State of New York.

Gift
Henry B. Joy
11-18-58
3-18-93

CONTENTS.

CHAPTER I.

The Preparation ---------- 5

CHAPTER II.

The milestone—The elegant young man—The collier—The rich lady ---------- 15

CHAPTER III.

The grog-shop—The rolling mills—The Universalist, 27

CHAPTER IV.

The new "relagin"—The hard father and his little daughter—The deserted homes—The stolen books, 37

CHAPTER V.

Book preachers installed—"Caught with guile"—The clenched fist—Review ---------- 49

CHAPTER VI.

Governor of West Virginia—Surprising desolations—The lodging—The dinner—"Blazing the trees" --- 57

CHAPTER VII.

The hunter seeking books for a Sunday-school—The first sermon—Clock pedlars ---------- 68

CHAPTER VIII.

The "Ironside" preacher and distiller—Wife and granddaughter ---------- 75

CHAPTER IX.

A church dignitary—"Have you let Washington into heaven?" ---------- 81

CHAPTER X.

The pistol—The surveyor's son—A public-house—"You have prayed plenty"—The pocket-Bible ---- 89

CHAPTER XI.

The summit of Cheat mountain—The "fellow that wanted to colport"—The sheriff's warrant—Wishing to be a *tract* agent ---------- 97

CHAPTER XII.

The wickedest man in the county—The bully—The shooting match—A gang of desperadoes ---------- 111

CHAPTER XIII.

A night on guard—Old Randal Lucas ---------- 119

CHAPTER XIV.

"No church, no preacher, no Sunday-school, no day-school"—A young lady's success ---------- 128

CHAPTER XV.

"No such place as hell"—The busy lawyer—A Trinity—The great work in L——, and in U—— ---------- 137

CHAPTER XVI.

A Pentecostal season—Service in a graveyard—A Seceder church ---------- 151

CHAPTER XVII.

The Spirit's blessing at C——, and near Marshall's Pillar, and at L—— B—— —Col. S——'s household, 163

CHAPTER XVIII.

Grieving the Spirit—Striking effects of the Anxious Inquirer ---------- 176

CHAPTER XIX.

Work of grace at L—— —The German professor—The wealthy young lady—"Do n't be offended"—A distinguished civilian ---------- 188

THE CONCLUSION ---------- 201

FIVE YEARS

IN

THE ALLEGHANIES.

CHAPTER I.

"It is not in man that walketh to direct his steps." In all my connection with the scenes here truthfully described, as in the training and discipline of earlier years through which I was brought into them, I have been *led in a way that I knew not.*

I was born on the border of Western Pennsylvania and Virginia, within the wilds of the vast range of the Alleghanies, where the howl of the wolf, the scream of the panther, and the Indian's tomahawk were my dread. In infancy my father died, and a few years later my pious mother. But God raised up a foster-mother, and in her family an intelligent Scotch female teacher, who made me her special charge during my first year at school. Here, in connection with faithful preaching from a tent in the woods on the Sabbath, and instruction in the log-cabin day-schools, I received those rudiments of education, and was indoctrinated in that sound system of faith and morals from which "old Scotia's grandeur springs."

Conscious of my ruin by sin and need of the "new birth," as set forth in old standard works of Flavel and Boston which I read, for three years from ten to thirteen, I was often deeply impressed as to the state of my soul. I attended constantly on preaching and the monthly examinations, committed to memory catechisms and scriptures, and wrestled with God in prayer that I might be truly converted and become a minister of the gospel; and sometimes I indulged a trembling hope in Christ.

But among the snares and flatteries of ungodly companions, my alarm and faint hopes of salvation gradually subsided. I was at length led to show my *manhood* by tobacco-chewing, card-playing, and even profanity. Next I was enticed to read works on Universalism, and for four years sought to stifle conscience by arguments to prove that all will be saved. Yet a still small voice was whispering, "The soul that sinneth it shall die;" and though jovial in company, when alone hell would seem to flash up before me in all its horrors. Two great powers were striving in my heart: one to lead me into deeper sin; the other crying, "Turn ye, turn ye; for why will ye die?" At seventeen I went with an ungodly young man into the then wilderness of Central Ohio, where for half a year I heard no sermon, hunted on the Sabbath, threw off restraints, and as it were dared the vengeance of God. Oh how astonishing the mercy of God, to continue to strive with such a rebel!

When I arrived at eighteen, I spent two or three nights in a week at the card-table, to "kill time" and drown the whispers of the Spirit. I thought of enlisting in the army, and then resolved to go to sea: but in the providence of God, a young woman just then engaged my affections; thoughts of the army and the sea were dislodged, and in a few months we were married, depending on our personal exertions for the means of support.

We rented a piece of land, and entered upon the scenes and responsibilities of real life. After six months, I was seized with acute inflammatory rheumatism, and the verdict of the physician was, that the disease was incurable, and I must die. Every feature was distorted with agony; and yet the agony of soul at the thought of being dragged into the presence of God with all my sins unpardoned was unspeakably more terrible. I saw that I had shut my heart against the calls of God's word and Spirit a thousand times, and that I deserved the deepest hell. I tried to pray, but there seemed to be no God to hear, no Saviour to intercede, no Spirit to comfort my lost and wretched soul.

As I was recovering, "The Afflicted Man's Companion," received from a friend, was greatly blessed to me, and I resolved by God's help to live the life and die the death of the righteous. The struggle now began in earnest. Such was my agony of soul, that I often went to the woods and rolled on the ground for hours. Most of those around me, for miles in every direction, were living in neglect of God; intemperance fearfully prevailed; there was not one religious friend to whom I could reveal the feelings of my heart. I tried to surrender myself to Christ, but in vain. A voice seemed to follow me continually, "He that is ashamed of me and of my words, of him will I be ashamed before my Father and his holy angels." I felt that a public acknowledgment of Christ and his cause was the only way of relief; but I shrunk from the duty, wishing to be a secret Christian, and go to the Saviour, like Nicodemus, by night. This distress continued for some months.

At length I was enabled to ask a blessing at my table, which seemed a hard task before my then irreligious wife; and after this it was a struggle of six months before I could summon courage to commence family prayer, even on a Sabbath evening. This duty was then performed, and peace of mind followed. After a few months I made known the state of my mind to the officers of a church some miles distant, and was admitted, though with many sore misgivings and fears that I had no right to the Lord's supper, and was self-deceived.

God graciously removed these doubts, and I felt the claims of Christ to do something for others. I first engaged in loaning such good books as I could get, especially The Afflicted Man's Companion, Doddridge's Rise and Progress, and Pike's Persuasives to Early Piety; feeling assured that no one could prayerfully read either of these books without being converted.

When I was in my twenty-third year, a devoted Christian settled in a very wicked community about five miles from me, where he started a Sabbath-school. I went to see it, and was greatly pleased with it. At the close, I was introduced to Mr. P——; and to his influence, under God, more than to that of any other individual, is to be traced all I have been enabled to do for the salvation of souls. He told me all about the management of a Sabbath-school, and how to get books from the American Sunday-school Union, which had just begun its heaven-born work in our country. I immediately set to work, raised five dollars, procured ten dollars' worth of books, and opened a Sabbath-school in my own house. The room soon became too small; but God put it into the heart of an irreligious neighbor to offer a larger room, where the school was continued for a year, and where I also held a weekly meeting, usually reading one of Burder's Village Sermons. More room soon became necessary, and a large school-house was built; and there, for twelve long years, the Sabbath-school and religious meetings were kept up, until nearly all the youth and most of the adult population in the neighborhood were brought into the church.

This Sabbath-school and that of Mr. P—— were the means God used to build up a good congregation in one of the most wicked and hopeless communities.

With these results before me, as soon as I heard of Colportage my heart beat with joy at the thought that the poor would soon have the gospel preached to them, and that thousands of children, untaught at home, would be reached by soul-saving truth adapted to their opening minds.

But the question came into my mind at

ence, "Who will go into these ignorant communities, and deny themselves the comforts of home, to do this work?" little thinking that God, by fifteen years training, had selected me for that very work in the Alleghanies.

An incident that occurred some years previous made a deep impression on my mind. The ecclesiastical body with which I was connected had requested the officers of vacant churches to visit all the families in those churches, and talk and pray with them. I shrunk from the task; but encouraged by Mr. P——, I entered on it with fear and trembling. By the time the first visit was paid I felt as if I should like to spend my days in such a work. Late in the evening of my first day I stopped at a house where the man and his wife were members of our church. A young man was present who was to be married in a few days. I had some acquaintance with him, and asked him if he had ever felt any concern about his soul. He said, "A little sometimes, but not much." I urged him to seek first the kingdom of God and his righteousness, and said to him, "For aught you know, before another morning you may be dead, or on a sick-bed from which you may never rise." At midnight that night he woke up sick. In a day or two I was sent for. He told me the moment he woke sick he thought of what I said, and felt that he should never get well. He lingered three months; but more than a month before he died he professed his faith in Christ. From that time till he died, he daily urged his ungodly, intemperate parents to repent and meet him in heaven. The father soon became much distressed about his soul; and a year after, he died a most triumphant death, committing his children to my care for religious instruction. Within a few years the mother and most of the children were united with God's people. All attributed their salvation to the exhortations of that son and those of us who attended him and his father. This encouraged me to try to do more.

On the morning of October 20, 1844, I rose in peace, with my happy little family around me; but a holy Providence ordered that in twelve hours my dear wife was to be in the cold embrace of death, and that her death was to be the first of a chain of providences to lead me "out into the highways and hedges."

The next Sabbath morning our pulpit was occupied by Rev. Mr. W——, who presented the moral and religious wants of our country, and tenderly appealed for laborers. At the close of the service I was introduced to him, and he accompanied me to the new-made grave of my beloved companion. The band that had bound me to my home was loosed. On Monday morning the preacher called on me again; preliminaries were arranged; and I was commissioned as colporteur for Western Virginia, consenting first to labor a short time among the colliers in Western Pennsylvania.

CHAPTER II.

I LEFT home for the field of labor assigned me on the first day of November, 1844.

On my way on horseback I came alongside of a young gentleman of very fine appearance. We immediately entered into conversation about the beautiful farms and fine improvements we passed.

When we had rode some distance, I observed *a mile-stone*, which reminded me of a promise made some years before, that I would never travel a mile or spend an hour alone with any person without talking on the subject of religion. I immediately set about to find something to make an introduction out of. The first thing that caught my eye was a very tall hickory pole, raised by one of the political parties of the time, and said I feared the political excitement was very seriously affecting the interests of the church.

The evasive reply of the elegant young man led me to suppose he was a gay, thoughtless young lawyer or physician, as I had discovered that he was an educated man.

I then observed to him that as we were providentially thrown together, and I had made a promise not to travel a mile or spend an hour with any one without speaking on the subject of religion, I hoped he had no objections to such conversation.

He said, "It is no doubt an important subject," but said it in such a way that I still thought he was an irreligious man.

I then observed that I felt a deep interest in young men, especially as the destinies of the church and nation would soon be in their hands. That the only safeguard of either was real piety. I then repeated the text, "Except a man be born again he cannot see the kingdom of God." And after preaching him a sermon from it near a mile long, he observed,

"Well, sir, that is very good theology."

The manner in which it was said led me to reply, "Perhaps I have run against a preacher."

"Yes, sir," said he, "I am a new beginner at it, and you have given me one of the best lessons that I have ever learned. I thank you for it; it needs no apology, and I hope God will give me grace always to do likewise."

Our journey as we continued it to Pittsburg was pleasant and profitable.

In the evening I reached the hospitable home of the Rev. Mr. J—— in the village of T——, near to the city. It had been arranged for his house to be my headquarters, and I shall never forget the nights I spent with him and his devoted companion. I thought him as nigh Christian perfection as man is ever raised in this world. Had it not been for their wise Christian counsel and earnest prayers, my faith and courage would have yielded when I came to look on my field of labor. My new work, to which everybody was a stranger, and to be done among strangers in the bustle of business and worldly excitements, seemed to be too formidable an undertaking. All nations seemed to be represented; scores intoxicated, and blaspheming God's holy name. And what added to the difficulty was, that my books did not come to hand for three days, leaving me that time to magnify molehills into mountains of difficulty.

But this delay was the most important part of my training. Those were days of most earnest searchings of heart, while such passages of Scripture as, "He that is ashamed of me and my words, of him will I be ashamed before my Father and his holy angels," were constantly ringing in my ears.

On the evening of the third day the box of books came. I had engaged a class-leader in the Methodist church to go with me the first day; but the sight of the box made me tremble, and so great was the dread of beginning the work that evening, that I resolved that if God did not give me strength by the next morning, I would start home and give it up. The night was spent without sleep. I can truly say I was in an agony till four o'clock in the morning. Then in a moment of time all my fears were gone, and I longed for the morning to come that I might begin my work.

By eight o'clock in the morning I called on Mr. S—— who was to accompany me, with my basket filled with good books and tracts.

In a few minutes we entered the first house.

They were Germans; very irreligious. We talked and prayed with them, and sold some books. They seemed pleased with the visit, and thanked us for it.

The next house we entered bore the brand of intemperance. The husband was sitting by the fire with a sore hand and red eyes. We preached to him "righteousness, temperance, and a judgment to come," till he trembled and wept like a child. He promised to drink no more, joined a temperance society that night, became a church-going man, provided for his family, and as far as I know has turned out well.

During that day we visited twenty-seven families, talked and prayed with all of them, and distributed near twenty dollars' worth of books. Many shed tears while we talked with them of Christ and salvation, and promised to attend to the "one thing needful."

Mr. S——, my fellow-laborer, was so stirred in soul with the day's work, that he said he must let his business stand and go the next day.

The next morning we started, full of zeal and hope. We met with many of the most wicked and degraded people that I had ever seen. Some listened to us with attention, while others treated us with contempt. Late in the evening, while we were visiting a row of board shanties, occupied by coal diggers, I was told not to venture into one of the shanties; that the man was almost a giant in size and strength, and a very dangerous man; that he was a terror to the neighborhood, and had beaten his wife very badly the day before. I replied there was the more need to see him, and I would go in. My friend would not even come to the door of the shanty, for fear of him.

The shanty was sixteen feet square, no floor but the earth; neither chair, table, nor bed except a bundle of straw in one corner. He was seated on a large block of coal at one side of the fire, and his wife on another block at the other side, while the children were lying on the ground playing between them. The woman's face bore testimony of the beating she had gotten the day before.

He was one of the most fiendish-looking men I ever saw. He was of enormous size, was clothed with rags, and did not appear as if he had been washed for months. He was as black as coal-dust could make him. I must confess it required all the courage I could summon to speak to him.

I approached him, and extended my hand, and said to him, "I have come to supply you with some good books to comfort you and point you to heaven. Have you a Bible?" "No," said he. "Can you read?" "Yes, a little." "Do you love Jesus Christ?" "I fear not, sir." I then urged him by every thing sacred to attend to his soul's salvation without delay; that death, judgment, and eternity were hastening on, and pictured to him as well as I could the awful consequences of dying in his sins. The tears ran down his blackened cheeks till the coal-dust was washed away below his eyes. I gave him a book, and prayed with him. He begged me to call again, and said, "You are the first man that ever spoke to me about my soul."

During this day we visited twenty-two families, and had religious conversation and prayer with each of them. Mr. S—— had become so deeply interested, that he said he must go another day.

The next day we concluded to visit a coal digger's boarding-house, said to be the wickedest den that was to be found in the whole district. I will not attempt to describe its character. We entered late in the evening, as this was the only time we could find the men in. The house was kept by an old woman and her sons, who worked in the mines and were notorious for their daring profanity.

When we entered the house several men were playing cards, others were lying on benches about the room in various stages of intoxication. My colaborer was a small, timid man, and seemed somewhat alarmed.

I introduced our errand by proposing to sell them some good books, which they declined even to look at. I then commenced a general exhortation, which had no effect more than pouring water on a rock. I then called on my friend to pray, as it was his turn, and we had agreed to lead in turns. This he did with great fervor, and was responded to by the men with vulgar songs, and such other behavior as I have never seen before or since.

At the close of his prayer I turned to the old woman and told her I was astonished at the mercy of God that permitted such a family to live, and portrayed the awful consequences of her meeting her household in hell. I drew every alarming picture I could summon from the Bible or the resources of my own mind. After some time the old woman began to weep, and she promised to attend the mission chapel the next Sabbath. After supplying them with a copy of Baxter's Call, and a number of suitable tracts, we left them.

The next Sabbath the old woman was at the chapel. A series of religious meetings began that day, and before its close, as my friend informed me, who was a worshipper there, the old woman and one of her sons professed religion.

One day we entered a room where a man was lying sick. We introduced the subject of religion to him. He ground his teeth with rage, and swore he did not want to hear any thing on that subject. I then began to inquire about his complaints, and to prescribe some simple remedies, and he soon became calm. After some time I remarked that afflictions did not come by chance, neither did trouble spring out of the ground, but they were all sent of God for some wise purpose. "Do you think so?" said he. "Yes," said I, "and for our good." He then listened attentively, and soon shed tears. Though he was very poor, he bought some books. I prayed with him, and left him, but not without many thanks and entreaties to come and see him as often as I could.

This closed the work of three days, in which time we had visited eighty-five families.

These three days were the most interesting days that I had ever spent. By the next morning I found my voice almost gone, and all my limbs trembling. The excitement of the work and intensity of feeling had prostrated me before I was aware of it.

After a day or two of rest I resumed my labors for three weeks, when I went home a few days.

I then returned to the same place, and spent a month in visiting new families and revisiting old ones; and I shall never forget the cordial shake of the hand that I got almost every day, when I would meet some one in the house or on the street whom I had before conversed with and supplied with a book or tract. Special services had been held in several churches, and quite a number had professed religion. One minister told me he had taken into his church forty, many of whom dated their first religious impressions to reading the books and tracts I had sold or given them, others referred to the visits as the means of their awakening.

There was one thing in the work which struck me with great force—the effect on Christian people. I tried as far as possible to get some good man to go with me in my visits. It was a great help to me and added to my success, and at the same time it stirred up many to work for Christ that had never done any thing before.

One instance I will name of a Miss L——, though she had been a worker. She was a lady of large wealth, and had a number of poor tenants living on her property. She heard of my work, and came to see me. At her request I went to visit her "parish," as she called it. I went at the set time, and she was ready to go with me, basket in hand. During the day we visited thirty families, and talked and prayed in every house. When my strength failed she took it up, and such entreaties to sinners I have seldom heard, and such prayers are seldom offered. During that day I found eleven persons that attributed their conversion to her efforts with books and tracts. She said she was a colporteur before, but did not know it till that day. Reader, go and do likewise.

CHAPTER III.

I NOW add a number of facts and incidents that occurred during these two months of labor.

There was a Mr. G——, a coal-digger, of desperate character, that I had been warned not to visit. I was told that he was such an abandoned character that he was hopeless; that he spent the most of every night in a miserable doggery, drinking and fighting. I had passed his house every day for some time, but did not feel satisfied with myself for neglecting it.

At last I felt constrained to call one evening; but he had not returned from his work. I had a long, earnest talk with his wife, who seemed very careless and wicked. All I could say made no impression on her. I gave her a copy of Baxter's Call, with the earnest request that she and her husband would read it. What followed I will relate as near as I can in his own words in a prayer-meeting in his own house about two weeks after.

"While eating my supper, my wife told me some man had been here and left a book, which he was very desirous she and I should read. I got the book to look at it, and read a few pages without much interest; but as I was very tired, I concluded not to go to the grog-shop that night. In the morning, which was Sunday morning, I felt inclined to go and get my bitters; but seeing the book, I concluded to read till breakfast, and then go. By the time breakfast was ready I felt pretty serious, and asked my wife if she would not like to go to church—a place we had not been in for eight years. She said she had no objections. I read till it was time to go, and began to feel somewhat anxious about my soul. I listened to the preaching with intense interest. I read the book nearly through that evening, went back to the church that night, and when those who desired to have an interest in Christ were called for, I came forward. A week after, I found peace."

He then added, "If it had not been for that book, I think myself and wife would have been in hell to-night. That gun was loaded," pointing to an old gun in the corner, "with a view of killing myself and wife near a month ago, and if God had not saved me, it would likely have been done before this time. I was a miserable man; life was a burden; but now I am happy."

This narrative brought tears to all our eyes, and joy to our hearts.

I visited some of the grog-shops around the village every day to supply their customers with temperance tracts. In the village proper, no liquor could be sold, as in all the deeds for lots there was a temperance clause that forfeited the property if liquor was sold; but all round the village the grog was abundant, and customers plenty.

Passing one of these drinking places one day I saw several customers in, and entered the bar-room with my tracts. The liquor-sellers had got to know me, and often looked daggers at me. A good-looking man, well dressed, and about half drunk, was approaching the counter to get a six-cent drink. Said I, "My friend, I can give you something for six cents that will do you much more good, and no harm." He asked me what it was, when I presented to him Baxter's Call.

I told him the liquor might kill him, and if he would read that book with prayerful attention, it might save his soul. He said he would buy the book if he had the money, but that he had only six cents to pay for that glass of liquor, which by this time was standing on the counter.

We both came up to the counter, when I laid the book beside the glass, saying, "Here is life or death for six cents." The grog-seller said I had no business to come there annoying his customers, and injuring his business. I urged the man at the risk of losing his soul to buy and read the book. The struggle seemed to be between life and death. At last he handed me the money, took the book, and went out of the room. I then handed the landlord a book worth more than the whiskey, and told him to read it, and then sell it to make up the loss. This is only a sample of every day occurrences in village and city colportage. Eternity only will reveal the results.

At the request of the proprietors of a large rolling-mill, I visited those in their employ.

Among them was a man that professed to

be a kind of Universalist preacher. He was a boss over a number of hands, and I was told was shrewd and fond of argument, and was doing much injury in propagating his opinions. Late one evening I called at his rooms. There was no one in but his wife. I conversed with her some time, and found her a pious Christian woman. I asked her about her husband. She burst into tears, and said he was a kind husband, but a wicked man; that he preached sometimes, and was a Universalist.

While I was urging her to labor and pray for his salvation, a fine-looking man, of a haughty mien and deportment, came in.

I arose and introduced myself, and asked if he was Mr. V——, the gentleman of the house. He replied that he was. I then told him I was a colporteur visiting from house to house, selling and giving books, and talking and praying with the people.

"Oh, I have heard of you about here for two or three days. I am a Universalist, sir; I do n't believe there is any such place as hell." I replied that it would be well for many of us if that doctrine was true, and asked him how long he had been a Universalist. He said about eight years; that his mother had belonged to the orthodox, and taught him in his early years about a terrible place called hell, and that he knew no better till about eight years ago. That for three or four years after he heard the true doctrine of the salvation of all men, he was troubled with those foolish prejudices; but for the last four years he had never had a solitary *pang* on that subject.

I replied that it was often hard to get rid of a mother's instructions and prayers; that it had taken the devil four years to silence his conscience, and get them put to sleep.

"Do you feel confident," I said, "that you are this moment prepared to enter heaven if you were to die?" "Yes," said he, "as certain as I am that the sun rises and sets." "Well," said I, "is not this rather a toilsome world to live in?" "Yes," said he, "it is, and I have a full share of it." "Then," said I, "why not cut your throat, and go right to heaven this evening?" "Oh," said he, "I have my wife to provide for." "Oh," said I, "cut her throat, and take her along." "Oh," said he, "that would be wrong." "No," said I, "if your creed is right, it cannot be wrong; and even if it should, you would be done with all the consequences of the wrong as soon as you were dead." He hung his head, and made no further reply. I told him I hoped that he had seen the fallacy of his belief, and would at once abandon such soul-destroying opinions. I sold him several books, and left him.

As the men worked by turns all night in the rolling-mills, and it was difficult to gain access to them, one of the proprietors proposed that he would join me to visit them all the next Sabbath, when they often gathered in groups to play cards and drink. Accordingly the next Sabbath morning we were joined by a theological student, and commenced going round the houses and rooms, near one hundred in number.

Late in the evening we entered the apartments of Mr. V—— and his wife. They were sitting reading new books, which I think were those I had sold them. I said, "Good evening, Mr. V——. I have come to talk with you again, and I am glad to see you reading those books. I hope you have changed your mind on religious subjects." "No," said he, "I am more convinced than ever that I am right." "Well," said I, "I want to ask you a few questions by the way of information, as you profess to have a near cut to heaven." Said he, "I am not going to answer any more of your questions. I don't like to be criticized." I told him I would only ask him easy questions; that I wanted to know what that scripture meant which speaks of a class of men who "shall not be forgiven, neither in this world, nor in the world to come." Said he, "I am not going to answer any more questions."

Mr. R—— said he would like to ask him one question. "There were two thieves crucified with Christ. He said to the one, 'This day shalt thou be with me in paradise;' where did the other go?" He made no answer.

We all three united in urging him to repent and believe in Christ, but he made no answer. At last I said, "Brethren, unless God will hear and answer prayer in this man's behalf, he is a lost man." His wife was weeping as if her heart would break. We knelt in prayer, and I think there were four earnest hearts lifted up to God. He sat still some minutes, but at last he knelt. When we rose from our knees the tears were running down his cheeks. I said, "Do you feel no 'pangs' now?" With a sob that seemed to come from his heart, he said, "I do n't know what has come over me." We then pointed him to the Saviour, and told him we believed his feelings were produced by the Spirit of God. Of all the penitents that I have ever seen, I hardly remember one who seemed so deeply moved as this man. During the time he remained in that place he seemed to be an entirely changed man.

One day, accompanied by the Rev. Mr. J——, we called at the office of a very fine-looking gentleman, and introduced the subject of religion to him. He was rather surly and sceptical. I proposed to sell him a book, but he declined, saying that he seldom read such books. At last I proposed to give him a copy of Nelson on Infidelity, and went on to say that it equalled any romance in interest. At last he said, "I have money plenty to buy books, and as you are so urgent about it, I will buy it, and read it; and if it is not as good as you say it is, I will give you a thrashing the first time I catch you." I told him I would run the risk of that if he would read the book carefully.

About ten days after we were passing again, and called on him. He met us in the most cordial manner. I told him I had called to see whether he would thrash me or not for the book I had sold him. "Oh," said he, "it is the best book I ever read. I would not take five dollars for it, if I could not get another like it." We found him deeply anxious about his soul. After a long talk with him, I told him I was about to close my labors there, and never expected to meet him again in this world, and urged him to meet me in heaven. With tears running down his cheeks, he said to Mr. J——, "Will *you* not come and see me again?" Mr. J—— said with tears that he would, and he no doubt did very frequently.

CHAPTER IV.

CALLING one day at a fine country-house in Western Pennsylvania, I found a prosperous Irish family of more than ordinary intelligence. I inquired if they wanted some good religious books. The father replied, "What kind of *relagin* do you teach?" I replied, "The holy catholic religion." "Ah, it's not the Roman-catholic relagin. What objection have you to the Roman-catholic relagin?" I replied that all that I desired was, to teach the people to repent and believe in the Lord Jesus Christ and to lead holy lives, and that I was not going about to argue with people about their churches. Still he insisted on my telling him what objections I had to the Roman-catholic church.

At last I told him they violated the second commandment by the use of images in the worship of God. But this he denied. I asked him to get his Bible and compare it with mine. He brought out the Douay Catechism to prove he was right, and told me that was his Bible.

I got mine; but he forbade my reading it, as it was a heretic's Bible. I insisted on having Bible authority for the use of images in God's worship. As the old man seemed to be at a loss to defend his position, one of his daughters, a beautiful girl, presented herself before me, and said, "I can give you Bible plenty for the use of images, and the good resulting from the use of them. What was it that Moses put up on the pole for the Israelites to look at when the fiery serpents bit them?" I explained to her that the brazen serpent was set up, not to be worshipped, but simply looked at as a type of Christ, to whom dying sinners may look and live. But all my efforts were in vain. As I left them, she was still asking me to repent, and come over to the true Roman-catholic church as the only place of safety.

A few days after, the Rev. Mr. J—— requested me to visit the town of S——, where he occasionally preached, and had made an appointment for me to address the people at night, preparatory to visiting all the families. He gave me a letter of introduction to one of his members, who lived a mile from the village, and who he expected would go with me. I came to his house near dark, almost frozen. He received me very coldly, and neither offered me food or company. I inquired the way to town, and soon left.

The night was dark, the snow deep, the cold intense, and I was an entire stranger in the place. As I rode along the street, every door and window was shut, till I came to a store. I tied my horse and stepped in, and found a large, fine-looking man sitting by the stove alone. By asking a few questions, I learned it was Mr. S——, the proprietor of the town. I told him I was glad to make his acquaintance. That I had come there at the request of the Rev. Mr. J——, to hold a meeting that night, and to spend a few days visiting his people and supplying them with good religious books, and I would be glad to have his counsel and advice as to the best way to do it.

Said he, "It depends very much, sir, on the kind of religious books you want to circulate here. I suppose you have the Confession of Faith of the Presbyterian church among them, and I can prove that it is full of falsehoods;

and more than that, I want you to know, sir, that I have made a promise to kick out of my house every man that comes in it that has graduated at Jefferson College, and studied theology at the Western Seminary." As he closed the sentence, he stood up before me, as if he was going to make good his promise. I requested him to wait till I should explain my object. I told him I had no Confessions of Faith, nor any denominational books; that they were all the books of the American Tract Society, and approved by nearly all evangelical Christians, and consequently not sectarian. And as to the other objection, I had never graduated either at Jefferson College or the Western Theological Seminary, consequently he was barking up the wrong tree. "Why," said he, "are you not a Presbyterian preacher?" "No, sir," said I, "I have not the honor to be a preacher." He turned instantly and walked out, leaving me alone.

I stepped to the door, and asked a little boy who was passing if there was a Mr. G—— living in the town. "Yes," said he, "he lives in the adjoining house." I stepped to the door, and was cordially greeted by an old acquaintance. In a few minutes I was seated at a sumptuously supplied table, which I very much needed; and an hour after was in a school-house, holding forth to the people, with my belligerent friend for one of my hearers. I visited all the town; but Mr. S—— carefully avoided meeting me, always turning away to shun me; but I supplied his family with a good stock of books.

At the close of my labors in that town, I entered a very hilly region of country, and stopped over night with a Mr. W——, an aged, infirm man, who sent his son with me the next day to hunt up the cabins of the poor. The son had spent some years in a roving life, and seemed totally indifferent about religion.

In the first cabin we called at, we found a young woman in the last stages of a decline. I have seldom seen any soul so full of joy and peace. She talked more like an inhabitant of heaven than of earth. While we spoke of Christ's love, and what he had done for her, I saw the tears course down my companion's cheeks. When we left her he said, "Religion is a reality."

After visiting a few more families, we came in sight of a beautiful farm, which lay in a valley. Mr. W—— said to me, "I will not go with you to that man's house. He is an unbeliever, and a shrewd fellow, and if you talk to him on religion as you have done to others, he will get mad, and insult you. His wife is pious; but I have heard him say that when the preacher came to visit his family he kept out of the way, because he did not wish to insult him; and he will certainly insult you, if you speak to him on that subject." Said I, "He has the more need to be visited. Such persons are the very ones I am sent to hunt up; but as he may take offence at you for leading me to his house, you may fall behind, and come up after me," which he con cluded to do.

As I approached the house, I got off my horse, and took my big saddle-bags, filled with books, on my arm, and stepped into the house. In a few minutes all the children were in. They were fine, intelligent children; and to my surprise, I recognized their mother as a once dashing young lady I had known well fifteen years before; but she had entirely forgotten me.

In a few minutes in came my travelling companion and Mr. C—— with him; Mr. C——'s face indicating great determination and firmness. I immediately began to hunt for a text to begin with, and chose a little girl of three or four years old, whom I called to my side. I began to tell her about Jesus, and what he did to save sinners, and how deeply praying fathers and mothers felt for their dear children, whom they would soon meet at the bar of God. I asked her if father and mother did not pray for her. By this time the mother and the oldest daughter were weeping freely. I asked the mother if she would not rather see her children converted to God than any thing else. "Oh, yes," she exclaimed, "it burdens my heart." I cast my eye round towards Mr. C—— and Mr. W——, and both were weeping.

"Mr. C——," said I, "do n't you feel concerned about the souls of this interesting group of children which God has given you to train up for him?" "Not as much as I ought to do." His heart was so full he could scarcely utter one word. Said I, "Are you not a professor of religion?" "No, I am not. I have been a very careless man on that subject. When I was a young man I was very much concerned for a while, but I fell in with wicked young men, and read bad books, and I have entirely neglected religion ever since. But I don't know what has come over me now."

"I trust," said I, "it is the Spirit of God that has touched your heart, and I beseech you now to yield to his divine solicitations; not to delay for one moment. If you resist the Holy Ghost now, he may leave you for ever, and then your doom will be sealed; but if you now give up all for Christ, you will find peace, and there may be joy in heaven among the angels this moment." He cried out in the agony of his soul, "What shall I do to be saved?" I urged him to enter that night on all the duties that God had enjoined on him; to read his Bible, and pray for himself and family. He pledged his word to me to do it. He kept that pledge. I prayed with him, sold him eighteen volumes of good books, and left the whole family in tears. He soon after joined the church; and Mr. W——, I was told, professed religion soon after, and attributed his conversion to a day's travel with a colporteur.

I held a prayer-meeting that night at the house of Mr. H——, a man of remarkable piety and benevolence. He told me of an incident that marked his whole life, and made him what he was. Said he, "I served my time with a hard master to learn the wagon-making business. I had engaged to go, the day I was free, some forty miles to work as a journeyman. The evening before I was to start, a good man gave me his advice, and at the close asked me if I had money to pay my way. I told him I had no money, but could get there, as I was going to walk. He handed me fifty cents, all he had, as a present. While on my way I met a poor miserable man begging. He told me he was starving. I gave him the fifty cents, as I had no way to divide it. Before I had gone many rods I found a silver dollar lying on the road, over which he had stepped. I said to myself, '*God sent this*,' and I determined to serve him all the days of my life; and he has blessed me ever since."

In a few days I commenced labor along the line between Western Pennsylvania and Western Virginia. The Rev. Mr. R—— took a deep interest in my work, and travelled more than a week with me. Our work made quite a stir among the people. The news spread that we were entering every house, talking and praying.

We set a day to visit a neighborhood that was noted for its wickedness. There were several families owning fine farms who never entered a church. On the day set, we took an early start. As we approached the first house, we saw all the inmates running to the barn. We knocked at the door, but no answer. We went to the barn; but before we reached it they were running across the adjoining field. We understood the cause, and came back to the house, and put in at the window Baxter's Call and a few suitable tracts, with the earnest prayer for God's blessing to attend the reading of them.

We went on to the next house, but it was

closed, and no one to be found. We here also installed Baxter and several other preachers through the window; and so on till we had visited six families. At every one of these houses the people either fled or concealed themselves at our approach. Mr. R—— pleasantly observed, as we were poor men, he thought the best thing we could do for our worldly interests would be to take possession of the property, for he supposed they would never come to dispossess us. Great fear fell upon sinners at our approach.

A few miles distant I held a prayer-meeting one night, and had a large crowd. At the close, I laid my books on the table, and told them that I would sell to any that wanted to buy. In a little time the man of the house told me that a man had *stolen* his pocket full; that he was a very bad man, and we should have a fight if we attempted to take them from him. Among them was a fine pocket Bible. So I concluded to let them go, and pray that God would overrule his wickedness for good.

Some weeks after, while visiting along the Ohio river hills among the wood-choppers near the same place, I called at a cabin, and found a woman in deep distress about her soul. She told me she had got a book that was the cause. That a man had sold it to a neighbor. They were the fourth family that had read it, and all were concerned about their souls. I found all the families she named, and the book thus blessed was a copy of Baxter's Call which that man stole from me and sold to one of these families.

CHAPTER V.

DURING my labors in this region I was frequently requested to visit G——, a town that had been laid out about the close of the Revolutionary war, and is noticed in the history of the Indian wars as being near the scene of some bloody struggles. It contained over three hundred inhabitants, but never had a church in it. A good man built one near by.

The Rev. Mr. R—— sent a notice that he and I would be there on a certain evening to hold a meeting. A few came. He preached, and I made a statement about my work, and told them I was going to visit the town to talk and pray with each family, and supply them with religious books. I had engaged a class-leader in the Methodist church, who lived a few miles distant, to go with me.

We entered the village the next morning soon after breakfast. The first four or five houses we stopped at we could find no one at home, and we soon found they were hiding from us. We could see heads out at the doors and windows as we approached the house; but when we would knock there was no answer. As soon as we understood the matter, I told my colaborer they should not foil us in this way; that I would install preachers in every house before I left the place. I immediately commenced pushing in the old hats that were stuck in the broken windows, and threw into the houses a Baxter's Call, Alleine's Alarm, or a Sabbath Manual, and some of the most awakening tracts.

We spent two days in this work. With all the skill we could use, we did not get into one third of the houses; but we put good books into every one.

Some few months after, a minister who was preaching near by found many interested about their souls. He held daily meetings for some time, and more than fifty professed faith in Christ; many dating their first religious impressions to the silent preachers thrown into their houses at the time of our visit. In 1861, on the railroad, I passed in sight of this town lying across the Ohio river, and instead of the old dilapidated village it was seventeen years before, it looked to be new and flourishing.

At the close of my labors in that community I went to B—— county, Va., at the request of Rev. Mr. W——, who had a large country charge and was laid up by bad health. He requested me, in addition to visiting all the families, to hold prayer-meetings among his people every night. This I did for one month, and God's Spirit seemed to be present at every meeting. Every one I talked with seemed to be moved by the Spirit. I sold more than $200 worth of books; and a few months after, more than one hundred persons were added to the churches. Mr. W—— afterwards stated that a large portion of them had been led to consideration by reading the books we scattered among them.

He often gave me directions where to go, and what kind of people I should find them to be. On one occasion he directed me to a neighborhood where he had four or five families living some miles from the church. The parents all professors, with large irreligious families, and no family altars.

The first family of them I called on, I soon

found to be but little interested about religion. I spoke with the father as if he were a devout praying man; but told him I had no doubt there were some prayerless families in that neighborhood; and that God had declared that he would "pour out his fury on the families that call not on his name." I spoke of the sad effect of such ungodly living on children, and urged him to try and talk with all his neighbors about it, and to go with me a day or two till we should try to wake up such professors of religion. His family were present. I saw his very soul was pierced.

I visited all the families the same way. God's Spirit seemed to stir every soul. In a few months after, the pastor was able to visit them, and found that each had established the family altar. Each one resolved that he would begin to pray in his own family, and then he could go and urge others to do the same. Neither of them supposed that I suspected them of living without prayer till they began to compare notes; and then they found I had talked to all the same way. They sent me their thanks by their pastor for "catching them with guile."

In another neighborhood, I was urged by a very good man to visit his brother-in-law, who he told me was a wicked man, and raising a large family like heathen. He told me that he was a gentleman in his behavior to strangers, and would treat me kindly; but to secure for me a kind reception, he sent with me a young man who was a nephew both of himself and of the gentleman. The day was extremely cold, and the distance some four or five miles. We visited several cabins along the river hills, and expected to reach his house about noon, and remain there till the next day.

About one o'clock we came to the place. It seemed to be the abode of plenty. We tied our horses, and entered a large front room. Mr. C——, the head of the family, was in it alone, shelling corn on a machine, keeping up a hot fire by burning the cobs. His nephew introduced me to him, but he scarce looked at me, spoke very little, and went on with his work, without asking me even to sit down. We both sat some time without a word being spoken, when the young man passed through into another room, where the family were talking. As soon as I got warm, I concluded to try and do my work and leave the house, as every thing looked rather gloomy.

He was a big, fierce-looking man. His countenance indicated that he was a very wicked man, which proved to be the fact. I sometimes thought it would be best to leave him without saying any thing, but my conscience would not let me do that. At last I said, "Mr. C——, I am engaged in distributing good religious books, published by the American Tract Society, and I have called to supply you and your family with them." I had scarcely got the words spoken, when he sprang right before me, with his fist clinched, and called me a horse-thief and robber, and every vile name that a vile tongue could use, interspersed with the most awful oaths I ever heard. He rubbed his fist under my nose, and swore he would smash my face into a jelly. I sat still for some time without speaking, in the hope that he would stop, that I might reason with him; but it was in vain.

At last I thought, if I am the cause of this man's sinning so much, I will leave him. I rose to my feet and said, "Mr. C——, if you will stop a moment till I speak, I will leave your house. I came here at the special request of Mr. E——, your brother-in-law, to try to do good to you and your family. And now, sir, I warn you, that if you do not repent you will perish. I leave a message from God to you on this table," placing there Baxter's Call and a number of tracts; "and if you reject them, they will meet you as witnesses on the judgment-day." The wicked man quailed, and tried to make apologies for his abuse of me; but I told him to ask God for pardon, and not me, for I was not in the least injured. I never saw the place or the man afterwards; but I heard he soon went to ruin. None of the family showed their faces during the interview.

Eighteen years have now passed since these labors were performed, and sufficient time has elapsed for all the dust and excitement to pass away; and on a calm review of that period of my life and labors, I look on it as the most important of any through which I ever passed: not in actual results, but in the development of a great system of evangelization, which has carried salvation to thousands who had never been reached by saving truth. A few had previously entered this field of Christian effort for the destitute, and done much, north and west; but this was the beginning of the work in the middle and southern states, which has reached millions of all classes and conditions, both bond and free. As to myself, I found it the best school I ever entered for spiritual and intellectual improvement, and if I have since been the instrument of any good to my fellow-men, the labors of the little time referred to prepared me for it.

At the close of this month's work, two gentlemen called on me one evening, and requested me to take a walk in the village of P——. I was soon led into a tailor's shop, and had my measure taken; and then from one store to another, till a fine new suit, from head to foot, was selected, costing near fifty dollars.

CHAPTER VI.

April 1, 1845, I commenced my labors in the town of F——, in Western Virginia. As soon as the object of my visit to that region was known, I received a cordial welcome from a large majority of the people, who did all they could to aid me in my work. Mr. P——, a young lawyer at that time, and since governor of Western Virginia, volunteered to go with me to every house in the town. His high position and universal popularity made the work pleasant and successful. In three days my buggy load of books were circulated in the village.

I immediately replenished my stock, and commenced my work in the country among the mountains. It was like a translation from sunlight into darkness—from a high civilization into one of ignorance and superstition, with here and there a family of wealth and refinement.

The very broken, rugged state of the country, with a sparse population, rendered it impossible for the people to support either schools or churches. Consequently in many isolated communities whole families grew up without any one knowing the alphabet, and very few places had preaching more than once in a month, and that on a week-day in some log cabin to a few women. I have visited as many as ten families in succession, in one case fourteen, without finding a Bible. It will hardly be thought strange that youth of both sexes were often found who could not tell who is the Saviour of sinners, and that when they were told of Christ dying for sinners, they would look incredulous and say, we live so much out of the way that we never hear any news. They often lived in small cabins, without any furniture but such as they made with an axe and an auger. All they raised to eat was corn and potatoes, with a few hogs; most of their meat being that of the various wild animals which abounded in the mountains. They were mostly kind and hospitable, and seemed to be sorry that they could not accommodate me better. I shall endeavor faithfully to describe one journey, which will represent many more.

About the time I went into that region, a new missionary circuit had been laid out by the Methodist Protestant church through a broken mountain country, where the gospel had never been preached; and the Rev. Mr. C—— was appointed to go round it once in each month, which required a ride of more than one hundred miles, most of the way by mere bridle paths.

He had been once or twice round the circuit before I became acquainted with him. As soon as he learned my business he invited me to go with him. He told me the people were without books of any kind, that very few could read, and that many of them were not half civilized; that at one house, where he spent the night, they cut off the skirts of his saddle to sole their moccasins, and at another the woman cut off the tail of his overcoat to make a pair of pants for a little boy. I agreed to go, and at the set time we filled each of our saddle-bags with little books and tracts, and our pockets with lunch.

The first appointment was some twenty miles distant, and we had to start the evening before. We stopped over night with a wealthy Christian family, and fared sumptuously.

The next day we rode twelve miles to the place where he was to preach. They had a church built of round logs. It had no floor but the ground, and was neither chinked nor daubed, consequently it was only used in warm weather. The house was full at the appointed hour. More than half of the congregation were barefooted, and but few had on them more than two garments. Most of the men came in with their guns in their hands, and a good supply of small game they had killed by the way. The guns were all set up in the corner of the church, and the game laid beside them.

At the request of Mr. C—— I conducted the service. The constant responses and loud amens indicated the deep interest they seemed to feel. At the close of the service I requested them to keep their seats, and told them I would go round and give each a tract or little book. More than half the families represented were destitute of the Bible. The tracts and books were received with very great joy, though few could read a word in them.

At the close we had to ride some miles to a stopping place for the night. We found the cabin small and destitute of any seats except stools. The beds were poles put through the corners, covered with the skins of deers and bears. Many of the spaces between the logs were wide enough for the dogs and cats to pass out and in at pleasure. The food was bread made of corn ground in a hand mill, or pounded in a hominy block. The meat was coon or opossum, and the coffee made of chestnuts. The night was spent in self-defence against unseen foes, and in dread of snakes. After partaking of a breakfast similar to the dinner and supper just described, and praying with the family, we left them.

Our appointment for that day was about twelve miles distant, with a constant succession of mountains to cross. We stopped at all the cabins by the way, which were about like that just referred to, with one exception; and as the house and family were different from any that I have ever seen, I shall try to describe them.

The cabin was about eighteen feet square; had been the birthplace of a large family;

had neither floor—except the earth—upper story, chimney, chair, table, or bed, except a pile of straw in one corner, and an old spinning wheel and loom. The family we saw consisted of the father, mother, and five daughters, no one of which, we supposed, would weigh less than one hundred and fifty pounds. Each of the females had on a single garment made of coarse linen, held on by a drawing-string round the neck, all fleshy and hearty, while we could not see any thing for them to live upon.

No one of them knew a letter in the alphabet, or who was the Saviour of sinners. They were children of nature isolated from the world, equally ignorant of both its vices and its virtues. We spent more than an hour trying to teach them the alphabet of Christianity, and then commended them to God. They seemed amazed at what we said; God only knows the results.

We reached the place where our evening meeting was to be held after one o'clock, exhausted with hunger and heat. The cabin was but little better than the one just described; it contained some kind of table and a few stools, but had neither door nor floor, and cattle and hogs ran into it to avoid the flies when they chose.

Mr. C——, whose patience was nearly exhausted, told the woman that we were almost starved, and to hurry and get us something to eat, and to make it as *clean* and as good as she could. The children were sent to borrow tools; a fire was soon blazing under an arbor made of bushes near the house; a pail of meal set beside it, waiting for the *skillet* to heat, out of which the hens helped themselves every time she turned her back to them. The children soon returned with a little coffee-pot minus the handle, and with a knife and a fork one prong lacking.

We were soon invited in to our dinner from under the shade of a tree where we had observed the whole process. The table was a block of wood, with four legs to hold it up, and a stool at each side for us to sit on. Some pet pigs were under it waiting for the crumbs: they tramped on our toes, which led us to kick them; but our kind hostess soon made the children catch them and confine them behind my back in a big gumm, a tub sawn off a hollow log, which treatment, from their noise, they seemed to dislike very much.

Soon after our meal was finished the people began to gather in to hear the gospel. The cabin was more than full, with the same appearance of the congregation as last described. We supplied all with books and tracts—in most cases with the first book they ever had. The night was spent much like the previous one, food and lodging about the same.

The next morning we rode nine miles to meet another appointment at eleven o'clock. By the time we reached the place I was so sick that I had to lie down, while brother C—— preached to the people from Jeremiah 6:16. At the close we supplied all with little books and tracts, and received many thanks. The dinner was set under a shed outside of the house, but the sight of it sent me out to the shade of a tree so sick that I could not stand on my feet.

I then told brother C—— that I should be compelled to make my escape to some place where I could get something to eat and take some rest; and asked him to take all the books and give them away at each appointment to the best advantage he could.

At two o'clock I was on my horse, which, happily for me, had been along the road before, and was suffering from hunger as much as his rider. In six hours he was standing at the steps of Mr. S——'s house, two miles from the town of F——, from which we started three days before. I was well acquainted with Mr. S—— and his family, having been frequently there; but fever had dethroned my reason, which did not return till I was taken in and my head bathed with cold water, and I had drank a cup of coffee.

It was three days before I was sufficiently recovered to resume my work. We had visited twenty-seven families, talked and prayed with them all, given them books and tracts, and held three meetings. One half of the people were without any part of a Bible. As for other books they had none, and not one in ten could read a word.

I have detailed this one journey of three days not only to show the condition of this portion of our country, but as little more than a fair representation of destitute parts of many states in the Union. If each colporteur of the Tract Society who has visited these dark, broken, isolated regions of our country for the last eighteen years, had kept a journal of all the ignorance and wretchedness he met, it would have been the most interesting missionary journal the world ever saw. Their reports would differ as widely as the reports of those whom Joshua sent out to visit the promised land. While some would bring in the rich clusters of Eshcol, others, with equal truthfulness, could say that the land was inhabited by giants, whose walls were ignorance and superstition.

I was often reminded in my journeys of the early pioneers of our country who went through the forests, tomahawk in hand, blazing the trees as a signal of their intended occupancy of the land at some future time. These visits were the Christian pioneer's way-marks, not blazed on the trees with axe or tomahawk, but blazed on the hearts of men in a state of nature by kind Christian words, and sealed with earnest prayer; while the books and tracts, including many Bibles and Testaments, were deeds of trust to those that faithfully used them; and many by them have secured a title to eternal life.

The books were like Jacob's well—the digger was gone—but they have quenched the thirst of many a weary traveller on life's journey, and their smoked pages are still crying, "Ho, every one that thirsteth," come and partake of the waters of life "without money and without price." A poor woman who had a small tract given her, on her deathbed had it brought to her, when she kissed it, and said, "This led me to my dear Saviour."

CHAPTER VII.

I VISITED an old woman, who told me that soon after she was married some one lent her Doddridge's Rise and Progress of Religion in the Soul, and that it was the means of the conversion of herself and her husband; that he had died happily some years ago, but she had never been able to get a copy of the book since. I then presented her with one, and she wept for joy. I asked her if she had a Bible; she said, "No;" that they had a Bible when her husband died, but some time after a little school was opened in the neighborhood, and she wanted her four little boys taught to read, but had no books nor any way to get them, and she had to cut her Bible into four parts to make each of them a book, and they soon went to pieces, and she lost her Bible. I then gave her a Bible, and her joy seemed complete.

On another occasion I sent a notice that I would be at a little church in a certain neighborhood to aid them in organizing a Sabbath-school, and to supply the destitute with books. After exhorting for some time, and arranging for the Sabbath-school, I distributed all my stock, and was about to leave.

A young woman came up to me, having just reached the place, and asked me for a book. I told her I had given away all that I had brought with me. She burst into tears, and said, "I left my babe, three weeks old, in the field where my husband was hoeing corn, and walked five miles in my bare feet to get a book; and now I am disappointed." In a few minutes an old woman who had seen seventy winters came to me with a crutch under one arm, and a cane in the other hand, and told me she had come two miles to get books for her sons, who were raising large families over the mountains, that were as wild as the deers. I returned soon, and gave the necessary supply.

One day a man entered my room wearing a hunting-shirt and moccasins, with a gun in his hand and a long knife hanging to a belt at his side, and asked me if I was the man that gave books to the poor people in the mountains. I told him I was engaged in that business. "Well," said he, "we live in an out of the way place, where we have neither schools nor preaching; and we met together last Sunday to see if we could not raise a Sunday-school, and teach our children to read, but all the books we could find was one New Testament; and some one said there was a man in F—— that was giving books to the poor, and so I have come to see you about it." I gave him all the light I could as to forming and conducting a Sunday-school, and added twenty Testaments, with fifty small volumes of Tract Society books, and some tracts. He soon had them all in the bosom of his hunting shirt, and I have seldom seen a happier man.

The next Sabbath the school was started. In six months a church was organized, and soon after a little church built, and a man of God was preaching to them once each month. That bosom full of books was the means God blessed to this result.

On another occasion I stopped over night with a good man, who related to me the following fact.

"A few years ago a minister came to my

house late on Saturday night on his way to preach at L——, about thirty miles distant. Finding he could not reach the place in time to meet his appointment, he told me if I would gather in my neighbors, he would preach for us. There were but a few families in all this valley, and so far as I knew, he was the first preacher that ever had been in it, at least he preached the first sermon. I sent my boys out and gathered in my neighbors. At the close of his sermon he gave every one a tract. Among the rest he gave one to a poor widow with a large family, but neither she nor any one of her children knew a letter. She took it home with her without any knowledge of its contents.

"The next morning she returned and requested my wife to read it to her, which she did. 'Well,' said she, 'it is a nice thing to read; I do wish I could do it.' She took the tract home, and returned the next day to have it read again; and during the reading, the tears ran down her cheeks. 'Oh,' said she to my wife, 'do you think I could learn to read?' 'Yes,' she said to her, 'no doubt you can.' So my wife got a New England primer we had, and went over the letters a few times with her. She took home both the primer and the tract. The next morning she returned again, and while the tract was reading, her face was lit up with joy, and peace came into her soul. In a few hours she was able to repeat the alphabet. 'And now,' said she, 'if you will only learn me how to put two of them together, and give them a *name*, I can learn myself.' This was soon done; and as soon as she went home, she taught her children all she had learned. In a few months she and her children could read all that was in the primer. We have now a good church here, and she and most of her children are members of it. She seldom sees a tract but with tears of joy she exclaims, 'If it had not been for one of these little tracts, I and my children might have remained in ignorance and sin.' "

One of the great difficulties I had to encounter was the large number of families that could not read. These I found every day. When I would show my books and urge them to buy, the reply was, "*Oh, none of us can't read.*" I soon saw the necessity of planning some means to remedy this evil, and began to establish little Sunday-schools in each neighborhood. I would hunt up the best reader I could find for a teacher, furnish them with a small library of books, give them the best direction I could how to conduct it, and set them to work. Although some of these schools were very superficially conducted, and in many cases there was nothing done in them but teaching young and old to read, still they had the effect of rousing the mind to the acquisition of knowledge, and preparing the way of the Lord. Many of these schools accomplished great things, and resulted in the establishing of little churches. Others seemed to fail, except so far as they woke in the minds of some a thirst for knowledge.

Some families I could not prevail on to take a book as a gift, for fear there was some trick about it. Clock pedlars had been through some portions of the country a while before, sold the cheap clocks at thirty dollars apiece, and took notes for the pay, which had been collected in many cases by distress-sales. They would tell me how they had been treated, and that they were afraid I should send some one for the pay. I often avoided this objection by lending the book, and writing on it, "Loaned till I call for it."

Another great difficulty we had to encounter with these unlettered masses was their prejudice against education. Almost every day I had to meet this objection: "Oh, I do n't want my children learned to read; it will spoil them. I have got along very well without reading, and so can they."

CHAPTER VIII.

I HAD now been about ten months in the colporteur work, and seeing the great necessity for scores of men to engage in it, I thought I could raise the salaries, and employ one or two others to carry it on. I soon raised $150 to pay a man for a year, and Providence directed me to a good man to do the work. I then succeeded in finding another good man, and raising his salary; and in one month, by the Divine blessing, I raised and paid over for the support of colportage $750, and these efforts were continued till the colporteur work was extended throughout the more destitute regions in all Western Virginia.

I had made an arrangement to visit R—— county, some forty miles distant, and spend a month in colporteur labor. On my way I had to cross a river by a ferry-boat. Two travellers crossed with me. When we mounted our horses on the opposite side of the river, one of them asked me if I was going on a long journey with such a heavy load on my horse over that mountain country. I told him I had my horse loaded with religious books, and some Bibles, and that I was engaged in supplying destitute regions with the word of life, and would soon lighten my load.

"Why," said he, "are there any families to be found without the Bible?" Yes, I told him, there were many in all parts of our country. "Well," said he, "I do n't believe there is a family in my county without a Bible." Said I, "What part are you from?" "From Green county, Penn." "How far," said I, "from the town of C——?" "Five miles," said he.

Four weeks ago, I replied, I was there, and made an address before one of the Presbyteries of the Cumberland church, in which I spoke of the destitutions of our country and our mode of supplying them, when the Rev. Mr. H—— followed me with a speech in which he said "he believed one third of the families in C——, in which we were then assembled, were without the Bible." Another minister present doubted it. I told them I was there to visit the town, and would begin the next morning. A good man volunteered to go with me. We spent three days at the work, and found that out of *one hundred and fifty-seven families, fifty-four* had no Bible.

On my way to R——, late in the evening I began to inquire for some place where I could spend the night, as the indications seemed to be that a hard night's lodging was before me. As I inquired at each little cabin, they told me that "Parson W——," a few miles ahead, kept lodgers. As these mountain miles are slowly measured by a tired man and horse, I did not reach "Parson W——'s" till near nine o'clock at night. When I entered his little cabin, he and his wife and granddaughter were at a supper of corn-bread and buttermilk. I asked for lodging, which was granted, and was at once invited to supper. As soon as the parson was done eating, he went and put up my horse.

On his return, I asked him if he had any pastoral charge. "Yes," said he, "I built a church on my own land close by, and preach there every other Sunday." We were soon engaged in a religious conversation, and my views of truth were soon tested. "Well," said the old parson, "I thought you was a

Methodist preacher, but I find I was mistaken; but I *guess* you are a Presbyterian, which is no better." Finding the old man belonged to what was called the *Ironsides,* or rigid Antinomians, I thought it quite useless to talk to him.

Before I could get rid of him he made me tell my business. "Well," said he, "you are going about plundering the country. It was the Bible, Tract, and Missionary Societies that broke up the country in 1837 and '38."

As I was tired, and proposed tc go to bed, "Well," said he, "there is a bed in that corner for you." "As you are a preacher," said I, "of course you have family prayer, and I would prefer waiting to join you in it." "Ah," said he, "every one does their own praying here." "Is it possible," said I, "that you are a preacher, and have no family prayer, when God has said he will pour out his fury on the families that call not on his name?" "Oh," said he, "you may pray if you please." Seeing an old family Bible on a shelf, I took it down, and read a part of the seventh of Matthew. I commented on the verse, "Strive to enter in at the strait gate," etc. The moment prayer was over, he said, "I do n't believe a word you said." I was soon in bed and asleep, being tired.

When I awoke there was a good fire, and the old man sitting beside it. I was up in a few minutes. "I am glad you are up," said he, "as there is another point I must discuss with you." In a few minutes I quoted proofs from the Bible too clear to be resisted; when the old woman, who was of huge dimensions, sprang out of bed in her night-dress, and presenting herself before me, said, "Do n't talk to that fellow; he is a Yankee, and he is setting traps to catch you." The old man soon disappeared to attend to his still-house and cattle, and the old woman and granddaughter occupied the whole front of the fire, making their toilets; the old lady, in her earnest conversation, frequently using a long wooden fire-poker in close proximity to my head.

As the granddaughter was sitting near me, completing her toilet, I spoke to her about her soul, and offered her the Dairyman's Daughter. This roused the old woman again; and the old man, returning about the same time, forbade her to touch the book. The girl cried bitterly, and said it was such a pretty book she did want it, and there was not a book except the old Bible in the house. The girl's tears prevailed, provided I would write a receipt in it that it was paid for, which was done.

As soon as breakfast was over, and my horse ready, I asked for my bill. "*One dollar,*" said the old man; "I make it a rule, when any of you Yankees come this way, to fleece you as well as I can." This man was rich; had a great distillery, and I was credibly informed would take a bottle of whiskey with him to the church, and at the close of his services tell his people what a fine run of whiskey he had just had, and to come and taste it.

About a month after, on my return home, I stopped to stay all night some few miles from there, when lo, Parson W—— had stopped to stay too; but as soon as he saw me, he ordered his horse, and left. I had told about my lodging with him; and as the laws of Virginia at that time imposed a fine of twenty dollars on any one who had no license charging for lodging, some one had told the old man that I was going to bring him before the court.

CHAPTER IX.

About this time an incident of peculiar interest took place. The Rev. Mr. Q—— had invited me to visit the town of C——, and I had set a day to be at his house. Late in the evening of the day appointed, I arrived in the town; and while driving along the street, looking for his house, I saw him standing on his portico, beckoning me to him.

As soon as I had alighted from my buggy, he gave me a cordial shake of the hand, and said, "You have come just in time to see and hear one of the greatest dignitaries in the state of Virginia." I observed that I was perhaps a little different from many others; that I would not go a square to see a great man, unless he was a *great good man.* "Well," said he, "he ought to be a good man; he 's the bishop of the Roman-catholic church for this state; and as he is the first live bishop of the *Holy Catholic* church who has ever been here, he is attracting a great deal of attention. He preached in the court-house this morning, and it was crowded; and he is going to preach here for several days and nights. He has one or two priests with him, and they have come to plant a church here. Will you go and hear him?" "Yes," said I; "if you go, I will go with you."

As soon as tea was over, we went to the court-house, and it was crowded. In a little time the bishop arose, and without any introductory services, gave out his text: "Thou art Peter, and upon this rock I will build my church; and the gates of hell shall not prevail against it." He went on to define "the gates of hell" as the various Protestant sects, and wound up by trying to prove that Peter was the first pope, and got the keys, and that the successors of Peter still held the keys, and no one could enter heaven without going through the Catholic church. His sermon was delivered with earnestness and eloquence, and made a deep impression, as very few of all present were well informed on those matters.

He made much for his cause out of the denominational strifes with which that region had been afflicted, and I heard many say "Amen" to some of his thrusts. He announced that he would preach the next morning from the text, "Search the scriptures, for in them ye think ye have eternal life, and they are they which testify of me."

We returned to brother Q——'s, and sat to a late hour consulting what we had better do. Here was a man of Jesuitical cunning, misrepresenting Protestantism before a community ill qualified to form correct opinions. I urged Mr. Q—— to contradict some of his false statements; and after praying over the matter, we retired.

The next morning, at the appointed hour, the house was crowded, though there were not one dozen Roman-catholics in the community. Owing to the crowd, Mr. Q—— and I got separated. I lost sight of him, and for want of a seat elsewhere, got up into a window. In a little while the bishop announced the text, "Search the scriptures," and also announced that he would preach at night from the text, "These were more noble than those in Thessalonica, in that they searched the scriptures daily."

The ground taken in this sermon was, that searching the scriptures by the common people had led to all the religious heresies in the world, and had raised up more sects than there were chapters in the Bible. That there was but one true church, and out of all only one could be right. That Protestants called Luther a great reformer, and he was told there were no Lutherans in that town; consequently, if Luther was right they were all wrong; and if they were right, Luther was wrong, and could not be a great reformer.

He said the Catholic church could not be wrong; that she was infallible; she was "the pillar and ground of the truth." He pictured the quarrels among Protestants in the most hideous manner, and described a heaven full of such uncongenial characters, till the picture was ridiculous; and I saw that many present were delighted with it.

At the close of his sermon, or tirade against the Protestant religion, he sat down. I rose up in the window, much excited, to see if the Rev. Mr. Q—— would not call him to an account, when I was much gratified to see the meek and gentle form of Mr. Q—— slowly rising about the middle of the house. Said he:

"Bishop, you said in your sermon last night that there were now two hundred millions of faithful Catholic children in the world, against which the gates of hell could not prevail. Will you be kind enough to tell us where they are?"

The bishop rose with a half-courteous and half-disdainful smile, and said, "You need not ask me such a question as that; the regions they occupy are all marked on your own Protestant geographies; your little boys in the streets can point you to them, where they have been marked in black lines," and took his seat.

"Well," said Mr. Q——, "I would prefer you would name the countries to which they belong."

He rose again with a most indignant frown. Said he, "I suppose it would be rather humbling to one who calls himself a preacher to go to the little boys for information, so I will name some, at least, of the countries that are Catholic: France, Austria, most of Germany, Hungary, and Poland; and we shall soon have England, as part of the church there is only separated from us now by name; and Spain and Mexico are ours entirely;" and he took his seat again.

"Well," said Mr. Q——, "do you think we should gain any thing as a nation by changing our Protestant religion for that of Mexico and Spain?" and he took his seat.

The bishop arose still more indignant in manner, and said, "I really cannot understand what you mean, sir, unless you refer to your boasted liberties in this country; but if that is what you mean, sir, I can tell you I would rather go to heaven from Mexico or Spain, than to hell from the midst of all your boasted liberties."

By this time the audience had become intensely interested. Said I, "Mr. Bishop, I want to ask you a few questions by way of gaining information. If I understood you right last night, you said your church was infallible; that it never had erred, and never could err."

He replied very indignantly, "I said, sir, that the Catholic church never had erred, and never could err."

"Well, sir," said I, "it was once right to put Protestants to death for their religion, and of course it is still right."

He replied, "That is a Protestant falsehood, sir; the church never put any one to death."

Said I, "Sir, I can prove what I say by the faithful records of history."

"Protestant authority—we could not admit such testimony, sir."

"Well," said I, "whether you admit it or not, the blood of martyred millions is crying for vengeance, and the day of divine recompense will erelong come."

After a number of questions from Mr. Q—— and myself of similar import, Mr. Q—— said, "The general opinion is that General Washington and General Jackson died good men and went to heaven. What is your opinion, bishop?"

He replied contemptuously, "Why, sir, we do n't pretend to know whether they are in heaven or not; those are the secret things that belong to God."

"Stop, bishop," said I, "you said last night that you held the keys of the kingdom of heaven in your church, and that to you it was given to open and shut the door; and I now demand of you as one of these doorkeepers, to tell us whether you have let in the immortal Washington or not."

In a few moments the call was coming from every part of the house, "Tell us whether you have let Washington into heaven or not."

The bishop tore his surplice off in a rage, and put out of the house with one or two priests after him—the crowd following him, and calling out, "Come back and answer the question about our beloved Washington." But he went on, ordered his horse, pronounced a curse on the place, closed his meetings, and left the town. The excitement of the crowd was most intense.

CHAPTER X.

I HAD now been in my second year of labor for some months, during which I had made some long journeys, and seen some hard service.

I made an arrangement with Mr. M——, a very intelligent gentleman whom I had employed a few months before as a colporteur, to accompany me. The whole tour required us to travel near four hundred miles. More than two thirds of the way the country was wild and romantic, the population sparse and rude. Few thought it safe to go unarmed.

On the day set I met Mr. M—— at C——, where he resided. To my surprise he had provided a pistol for each of us. With some persuasion I took one, but soon got it to the bottom of my saddle-bags.

The first day we reached W——, where we found a young preacher who had been waiting there some days for an escort over the same route, fearing to travel the road alone. We all started in company early the next morning, with the understanding that we had to reach G——, a new county-town thirty miles distant, or lodge in the woods. Nothing special occurred that day, except that an enormous rattlesnake crossed the road before us and frightened our horses. We called at the door of all the cabins we saw, and preached Christ to the people, and gave them books. We reached G—— late in the evening, and found a pious lawyer who had just moved there, and owned the only Bible in the place. There were not a dozen families in it. By breakfast-time the next morning we had supplied him with a neat Sunday-school library, which he used to great advantage.

We were told we must ride thirty-five miles the next day, over mountain paths, to reach a place of lodging—that there was one house at thirty miles, but by all means to avoid that house. The reasons I cannot give; nor an account of the dinner we *tried to eat* that day.

As the weather was excessively hot, we left G—— by six in the morning. We soon overtook a young man who was going some miles our way, and agreed to be our guide as far as we went together. We found him totally ignorant of sin, or a future state. He did not know whether he had ever seen a Bible or not. Though he had heard men preach, and seen them with a book in their hand, he could not tell what book it was. He told us his father was a county surveyor, and, he thought, a member of the church. I gave him a Testament and some tracts, which he looked at with amazement.

About ten o'clock we came to a number of men at work cutting timber out of the road, that had been blown down by a storm. On inquiry, we found eleven families represented, only one of which had a Bible. One or two others had lost their Bibles by having their cabins burnt. We supplied all with books, and left one or two reading for all the rest.

The want of dinner and the excessive heat of the sun brought on me sick headache, and by four or five o'clock I could scarcely sit on my horse. I told my companions it would be impossible for me to reach the house we were directed to, and let the consequence be what it would, I should be compelled either to lie out, or lodge in the vile den of which we had been warned. The brethren seemed much alarmed, but said they would not leave me. Several times I had to alight, to prevent falling from my horse. Being thus detained, we only reached this dreaded place about sunset.

There was a very large grazing farm, and a large double log-cabin about the centre, with every appearance of plenty. As we drew near the house we saw quite a number of men at work haying in a large meadow. Every one seemed to be drunk. Such swearing and hallooing I had never heard. Our prospects looked gloomy.

We rode up to the door, and found the landlord under the same influence as those in the field. When we asked for lodging he seemed glad to have customers, and soon had our horses cared for.

In a little time all the drunken rabble on the place were gathered to the house, but such a set of men I have never seen before or since. Supper was soon ready, and all invited in. The food was very rough, but abundant. I was too sick to partake of it.

After supper I told the landlord that I was very sick, and must go to bed; but as we were all religious men, and accustomed to pray in our families night and morning, if he was willing, we would have prayers. The very announcement produced silence in a moment, as if some strange thing was about to happen. I requested him to bring all into the house that would come, and in a few minutes the house was well filled. I called on one of the brethren to read and pray; and soon after I was in bed, unconscious of all around me till morning, when I awoke as well as usual.

As soon as we were dressed I called on the old man to get our horses. "Oh no, you must stay for breakfast, and pray again," said he. "Well," said I, "if you will bring all in to prayers now, we will attend to worship with pleasure." In a little time the whole household was present. I read a portion of Scripture, and made the most earnest exhortation I could possibly do, and prayed. A more solemn audience I never addressed.

As soon as breakfast was over, our horses were ready, when I asked the old man for our bill. "Not one cent, sir," said he; "you have *prayed plenty* to pay for every thing you got. Every time you come this way stop and get all you want, and pray, and it sha'n't cost you a cent." We supplied all present with a book or tract, and left well pleased on the whole with our visit.

During the day we called at all the cabins on our way. At one I found a man who told me he was seventy years old, had seldom heard a sermon, but that he had felt much concern about where he would be *in the next world, if there was one.* He said he never had a Bible, but would like to get one very much. I gave him a Testament and tracts. He seemed very thankful, and listened with great attention to all I had time to say.

At another house the woman told me they had a Bible, and plenty of religious books. I asked to see what kind of books they were. When she presented the stock, it consisted of an old copy of the history of George Washington. She believed it to be a Bible, as no one about the house knew a letter.

The same day we met a very aged man riding on a poor little pony, with a small bag of meal under him. I handed him some tracts, for which he was very thankful, when the following dialogue occurred.

"Have you any preaching in this mountain country?" "Sometimes we have." "Are you a professor of religion?" "Yes, I have been a member of the church forty years." "How are you supplied with religious books?" "Well, we *have n't got none* but two or three spelling-books that I sent for many years ago to teach my children how to read." "Have you no Bible in your house?" "No, I never had one. I have been trying to get a Testament for some time at the store; but it costs seventy-five cents, and I am not able to raise the money." This was the regular price of a small Testament in that region at that time, and seldom to be got even at that price.

Said I, "Is it not hard to live the life of a Christian without the Bible?"

"Yes," said he, "but I can't help it; for even if I was able to buy one, it could not be got nearer than C——, which is forty miles distant. I never expect to be rich enough to buy a whole Bible."

My soul was stirred within me, and I drew

out my pocket Bible, a fine copy which I had received as a present, and gave it to him. He looked for a moment at me with surprise, when the tears gushed from his eyes, and he exclaimed, "I am now rich and happy." This man was seventy-five years old, and trembling on the brink of the grave. This is a true picture of many cases found by colporteurs. I never felt so well paid or so happy as when I gave that man my only Bible.

During this whole tour of five weeks' travel, many a scene similar to those described occurred; while, on the other hand, I visited villages and towns where I found fine churches and able ministers, with highly cultivated pious congregations. In this tour I raised over $500 in donations, and employed three excellent colporteurs, one of whom labored nine years. I met the most cordial coöperation from Christians and philanthropists everywhere I went. All said, "This is just what we need in this sparsely populated mountain country."

CHAPTER XI.

WHILE on this tour I visited the town of L——, near the centre of Western Virginia, and made arrangements to remove there in a few weeks. There are few towns of the size which I have ever visited where I have met with a more noble people. There was wealth, intelligence, and the highest degree of refinement. This town became the centre of my operations for three years.

The distance we had to go in moving there was about one hundred and fifty miles, up and down mountains most of the way, with scarce any thing like a road in many places: a family of five, two of them children, in a one-horse carriage, with the necessary equipage for such a journey.

On the afternoon of the third day we began to ascend the Cheat mountain, which required nine miles travelling to reach its summit, and eight miles down the other side to its base, with only one house all the way, and that on the top of the mountain, called at that time "the mountain house of entertainment." It was a large rude log-house, without comfort. By the time we reached the top of it I found my horse very much fatigued, and the sun about setting. We concluded we could not descend the mountain that night with safety, as there was no moon, and the whole way was through a dense pine forest.

When we came to this house on the very top of the mountain, we found a number of covered wagons that belonged to families moving westward, and a crowd of people of all colors about the house. I asked for lodging. "Yes," said the landlord, "lodging plenty!" My family went into the house, and I went to see my horse taken care of. On my return I found them without any place to sit down. After looking through the house, and finding but two or three apartments, and such a crowd of people, I asked the landlord how he would lodge us all. "Oh," said he, "you can lie down a few at a time, and soon as you get asleep I can stand you up against the wall."

Though it was in September, and very warm in the valleys, yet it was cold on the top of this mountain, and we were all shivering. I asked the landlord, who by this time was playing the violin for our entertainment, to make us a little fire. But there was neither wood nor supper. The females were stowed away in one room for the night, and the rest lay on the floor or sat by turns till the morning came.

As we had no toilet to make in the morning, we were on the way down the mountain at an early hour. The first house we reached was a log-house, where they kept entertainment. All was neat and clean. We called for breakfast; and while it was preparing, we had our morning devotions, which had been noticed by the landlady. When we came to our excellent breakfast, she asked me to christen her children, of which she had quite a number. I told her I was not a preacher, and had no authority to administer ordinances. She insisted most earnestly that I must do it; that no one had ever prayed there before, and she did not see any reason why any praying man could not christen children; that they had been living there for years, and never heard a sermon or seen a preacher as they knew of; and if I would only do it, they would not charge me one cent for breakfast. After preaching them the best sermon I could, and giving a good supply of little books, we went on our way. In two more days we reached L——, our place of destination, in safety, and in a few hours had a house rented and were living in it.

For three years I travelled almost constantly; sometimes in a buggy, but mostly on horseback, making from six to eight thousand miles each year, distributing tracts and books in cabins and mansions, collecting money, and employing men, till I had the co-operation of *over fifty colporteurs.* The many interesting facts and incidents which occurred during these years would fill a large volume. A very few of them I shall attempt to relate.

A Mr. W——, whom we had employed for some years, a man of much more than ordinary piety and qualifications for the work, while visiting in the mountains, came to a poor cabin occupied by a man, his wife, and an only son. They were very poor. The father made his living by grubbing, and took the boy with him to pick the brush, he being at this time about sixteen years old. They carried home their wages on their backs, mostly in some kind of food. The mother made what she earned by her spinning-wheel; and while at that, had taught her son to read the Testament, though she was not religious. Mr. W——, after talking and praying with them, gave this boy a copy of Baxter's Call, which was the means of his conversion. Before he could join the church, the neighbors aided in getting him a suit of clothes.

He immediately set about to improve himself in every possible way. There was no school near; and if there had been, he had no means to go. His first efforts in learning to write were, by copying the letters out of a book with his finger in the snow. He borrowed and read all the books he could get, and attended a little church where there was preaching once each month.

About two years afterwards I received a letter by some private way from this same boy, D. W. S——. On opening it, I made out its contents with some difficulty. It was an application to become a colporteur. In the letter he referred me to the Rev. Mr. R——, who lived in town. I went to him, showed him the letter, and asked him if he knew the writer. He laughed: "Yes, very well; I received him into the church. D—— is a good boy, but he is without education, and knows nothing of the world; he has never been ten miles from home in his life."

I wrote the young man a kind letter, saying I hoped he would make a colporteur some day, and advised him to go to school a while.

The next thing I heard from him was a rap at my door. When I opened the door, an awkward-looking youth near six feet high stood before me, with the same suit of clothes on him he had got over two years before. The pants were several inches too short, and the coat-sleeves as deficient; indeed, the coat was little more than a big patch on his back. Said he, "I am the *fellow* that wrote you a letter about wanting to *colport*, and I have come to see about it." I invited him into the house. He was all in a tremor of excitement. When I opened the parlor door he looked in with amazement, and in walking to a seat avoided stepping on the white spots in the carpet, which was the first one he ever saw. He was so embarrassed he could scarcely speak.

After talking a little while about crops, etc., he became composed. He then told me his desires to do good, and all about his conversion, which was entirely satisfactory. As it was late in the evening, I invited him to stay for the night; and by the time we got his poor old pony of a horse, not worth five dollars, put away, tea was ready. When he sat down he looked confused. I had much conversation with him that evening. At length I invited him up stairs to bed. On the way up he held by the railing to avoid treading on the narrow carpet in the centre.

In the morning he was up whistling psalm tunes bright and early. As soon as I was dressed I called him and told him I had reflected over the matter very carefully, and had come to the conclusion that his want of education and knowledge of the world would not justify me in employing him.

I saw his countenance change in a moment and the tears start in his eyes. "Oh," said he, "*I do want you to give me work, for I do feel that all I want to live for is to work for Christ.*"

I cannot describe my feelings as he uttered these words. Here was a depth of devotion beyond any thing I had met. After some minutes' silence I said to him, "There is a region of country on the head-waters of the Elk river where there never has been any preaching; if you will go there a month without any commission, I will see you are paid."

His countenance was changed in a moment, and lit up with joy. In less than two hours I had a pair of colporteur's saddle-bags filled with books and tracts, and he was on his journey to that destitute region, some forty miles distant. Soon after, some stock raisers who had been in that region buying cattle, told me they heard that the Tract Society had a great man out there; that the people were wonderfully pleased with him; that he was giving them books, and teaching them to read them.

At the end of the month he returned, all his stock had passed into the hands of the people, and he gave me a glowing account of the people's wants and his success. He said it would take another month to get over that region, and he wanted to go back. After aiding him to dispense with his boy clothes, I started him with another load of books, cautioning him to avoid showing off his new suit as much as possible.

Another month's work was done with great success, when he returned almost a new boy in his whole appearance. He had gained confidence by being constantly among people that did not know as much as he did.

I then had him commissioned for P—— county, a very mountainous region, and very destitute of the means of moral improvement. In a few months he had visited every family in the county. In many families the bare mention of his name will start tears in the eyes of the people, and the tracts that he distributed have been sewed together and covered with deerskin as remembrances of the man that left them.

Often through the day when he would come in sight of a cabin, he would alight from his horse and kneel in the woods and plead with God for success in his visit.

He next visited the counties of M—— and R——, two large counties, with remarkable success. By this time he became a fine-looking young man, and by his constant application to reading the books as he rode along, he had become an intelligent, spiritual Christian.

We then sent him to the large county of P——, where there was in portions of it a high degree of intelligence and refinement.

In a few months he was licensed to preach the gospel. He married a lady of high moral worth, and settled in the county of H—— over four weak churches. In two and a half years he received over two hundred persons into the church on profession of their faith; then took typhoid fever, with which he soon died in the triumphs of a living faith.

Since his death I have met with five young men, who are now ministers of the gospel, who had been led to Christ by his labors, all of whom speak of him as an extraordinary man in point of piety and usefulness.

Here was a boy that in all probability would have lived and died in ignorance and sin if he had not been found by a colporteur.

He has often put his hand on my shoulder, and said with tears in his eyes, "Brother C——, if it had not been for the Tract Society, I should have been a poor grubber to-day, on the way to death and ruin."

The great secret of his success was his untiring zeal and industry. He read and studied on his saddle; the shades of the forest were his closet in the summer, and the cleft of some mountain rock in the winter. His congregations were mostly ignorant families, and his rostrum a three-legged stool in the corner. All his talents were put to use in the Lord's work, and no doubt he has his reward. Reader, go thou and do likewise, and receive a like gracious reward.

On a Saturday evening while on my way to meet a Sabbath appointment, while descending a mountain, I met a man on his way home from mill, and offered him some tracts. "Oh," said he, "they are of no use to me, for I can't read, and I have no one about me that can." I asked him if he had a family. "Yes, I have a wife and seven children." "It is a great sin," said I, "for you to raise a family in such ignorance."

"Oh," said he, "there is so much harm in books, they are better without them." I handed him two or three tracts, and told him to get some one to read them to him. One of them was, Fifty Reasons for Attending Public Worship. He took them, and when he got home showed them to his wife. "Oh," said she, "we will be ruined now. I 'll bet that is a warrant that Middleton has got the sheriff to serve on you, and we will lose our land." They spent a sleepless night, and early next morning they went to the nearest neighbor and told him they had got into sad trouble about their land; that Middleton had served a warrant on them, and here it was.

The tracts were presented to a man who was a class-leader in the Methodist church, and was my informer near a year after this occurrence. He took the first one, "Fifty Reasons for Attending Public Worship." "Well," said he, "this is a warrant, but not sent by Middleton, but from the court of heaven. God has sent you this, as you never go to church; and now you see how you have exposed your ignorance by not being able to read, not knowing the difference between a sheriff's writ and a religious tract; and I do hope you will now attend church, and have your children taught to read." "Now," said my informer, "this man and his wife are both members of the church, and they are sending their children to school as the result of the influence of those tracts."

On one occasion I left home by a stage-coach before daylight on a long journey. We stopped after ten miles to take other passengers. As usual, the way-bill was taken into the stage-office to enter their names. A man was in the office who had travelled near one hundred miles to see me at L——. Seeing my name on the way-bill, he asked if that was the man that was the *tract* agent. About that time I stepped in to warm myself and distribute tracts, when some one acquainted with me told him I was the agent. He then told me how far he had come to see me, and how near he was to miss me, all the time interlarding his conversation with oaths, to the great amazement of all present who knew the nature of my work. When he was through, I told him I would tell him the nature of the work in a few words: that he must get a good horse and a large pair of saddle-bags, fill them with books, and ride over these rugged mountains, and live on hard fare. With an awful oath he said he could stand all that with any fellow about the diggins. In addition to that, said I, you must read the Bible, and pray at every house. I never saw a man so utterly confounded, while those present were convulsed with laughter. I gave him a few tracts, and talked to him till he wept like a child. Although I never heard of the man again, I have hope that the conversation was not in vain.

CHAPTER XII.

About this time I held a Colporteur Convention in C——, in which a number of colporteurs were present. The meeting was one of deep interest. Many facts were brought out in relation to the wants of that region, and the good resulting from the work, that were of the most cheering character.

During the three days of our meetings, an old man was present who was but little known to any that were there. When about to close the convention, I said that if any one present wished to give us a word of advice or exhortation we should be glad to hear it, when this old man rose, trembling with diffidence, and said:

"As soon as I heard of this meeting I made up my mind to attend it; and now I want to tell you what this Society has done for me. My name is C——. Ten years ago I was considered the wickedest man in this county. I was a profane drunkard. One day while at S——, about four miles above this place, old

Mr. R——, who was always distributing tracts, handed me one with the word *Eternity* in large letters at the head of it. I was the worse for liquor at the time, and on my horse to go home, which was about fifteen miles distant. On my way I took the tract out of my hat to read it. My attention got fixed on the word *Eternity*, and I became alarmed about my state as a sinner. By the time I got home I was nearly sober. I read and reread the tract till I had it committed to memory. For near two weeks I had no rest. At last my distress became so great that I did not want to live. One day I was tempted to go away to the woods and destroy myself. While there I thought of praying, for the first time, and fell down on my knees and cried, 'God be merciful to me a sinner.' In a moment I felt relief, and went home with a joyful heart, and told my family all about the matter. I read the tract to them, and began to pray with and for them. In six months I had a little church built on my land, and a missionary there to preach once each month, and myself, wife, and six of my children and eight servants were members of it;

and here is five dollars, all the money I have in the world, to aid in giving good books to others." All present were bathed in tears at this recital.

As soon as he was seated, another man arose and said "he supposed all present had heard of Father B——, who died a few weeks ago, and many, no doubt, remember when he was a terror in the community. He had remarkable bodily powers, and could whip any man in all the country round. When the county of L—— was laid off, there was a violent contest about where to build the court-house; and the two parties agreed that B—— and another bully should decide the matter by a fist-fight, and B—— gained the site where that court-house now stands. He was often brought up at the court for assault and battery, and had crippled some men for life. Judge S—— on one occasion, when passing sentence on him, said, 'B——, you have become too bad a man to live, and if ever you come before me again convicted of crime, I will make you suffer for it most severely. If you would improve the mind God has given you, you might be a blessing to the world;

but now you are a disgrace. Here is a tract, 'The Fool's Pence;' take and read it, and may God lead you by it to be a better man.' That tract was the means of his conversion, and for the last fifteen years of his life he was one of the most successful preachers in South-western Virginia."

Another fact was brought out at this meeting by the Rev. Mr. W——, who labored for some time as a colporteur in the county of W——. He entered a large settlement where there never had been any preaching, schools, or distribution of books. The Sabbath was the special day for frolicking and dissipation. In the house where he lodged on Saturday night, the family were busy preparing to go to a shooting-match the next morning. All he could say had no effect on them. After praying God to guide him in his duty, he determined to go with them. When they came to the place, a large collection of all classes were present, with a great number of articles to gamble for in different ways. He told them, as it was the Lord's day, he would unite with them in prayer for God's blessing. He prayed earnestly, and then told them that if they would give him their attention he would preach to them. They seemed confounded at this remark, and all remained silent as death. He announced his text, and preached with unusual liberty. The attention was solemn, and they looked at one another with amazement. He then distributed among them his remaining stock of books and tracts, and as he was very unwell, went home. Soon after the news spread that some people in that region were concerned about their souls. A preacher visited them, and soon had a good congregation gathered, and over twenty converts. Sunday frolicking was abandoned, and many were led to observe the Lord's day.

The same man stated another fact, which occurred in J—— county. While visiting in one of those sparsely populated regions, he came to a very large farm. He found the family to consist of the father, mother, and twelve children, the youngest about eight years old. The man was wealthy in land and stock, but to his surprise no one knew a letter in a book. After talking to them about their relations to God and eternity, he asked the father why he did not have his children taught to read. The old objection was raised at once, that they learned enough of *bad* without books; that he had got along very well without reading, and so could his children.

He then began to read to them, showed them the pictures in the Alphabet of Animals, and read them some account of them. Several of the children said, "Oh, I wish I could read." He then gave them one or two books and some tracts. A few months after he was coming back the same way, and called to pay another visit. "Well," said the old man, "you have give me a *purty lot of trouble by leaving them books here.* I had no peace till I got a man to come and *larn* them to read them." So sure enough the teacher was there, and now they bought more books freely.

In travelling through a wild mountain region, where I was a total stranger, I came to a small village of about a dozen houses, with a little store and tavern. Before I reached it, I heard men hallooing in the most boisterous manner. When I drove up weary to the public-house, I was surrounded with such a set of savage-looking men as I never had seen before, and all intoxicated. Every man had on a hunting-shirt, with a belt round him, to which hung a long butcher-knife. I felt afraid of the men, I must confess, and would have been glad to have been elsewhere, especially as my buggy and trunk seemed to attract rather too much attention.

After I had got food for myself and horse, and laid round some tracts as quietly as possible, I started, hoping to reach a point near twenty miles distant that night. Some part of the way I was told the road was very good, but mostly rough and mountainous.

As soon as I was out of sight, I drove rapidly, and made the first five miles in an hour, when I began to breathe easier.

But all at once I heard the most unearthly yelling behind me that had ever greeted my ears. My horse was frightened, and tried to run off. In a few moments I heard the clatter of horses' feet, and concluded all was over with me. In a moment I was surrounded with some eight or ten of the most desperate looking men, and told to stop; that they wanted to know what I was loaded with. I told them I was loaded with good religious books, which I was distributing among people that had none I was then ordered to give them all up to them, and they would scatter them on the other side of the mountain, for there were no books over there. I told them I knew they were too generous to take all that I had.

I then told them to listen to me, and I would tell them what the books taught. So I began and preached them the most earnest sermon that I ever preached. One of them said, "Give me your hand, sir, for I never had a preacher by the hand in my life." I held his hand firmly, and preached on, although the muzzle of his gun was frequently in very dangerous proximity to my person.

It was evident they began to feel uneasy under my wayside sermon, and for fear they would leave me without tracts, I began the distribution, and gave each one a number of the most suitable I could find. They invited me to come over the mountains and preach, and I would get plenty to come and hear me. Some of those tracts were found more than a year after by one of our colporteurs, carefully preserved and highly prized.

CHAPTER XIII.

Another case that seemed more threatening than the last mentioned, occurred soon after in the county of G——. I was on my way to meet a Sabbath appointment. About two o'clock I came to a river which was much swollen by the late rains. The man who kept the ferry-boat lived on the opposite side of the river, where some four or five men were pitching quoits and making a great noise. I called a number of times before they even condescended to answer me; and when they did answer, it was with curses, telling me they would come when they were ready. I had then sixteen miles to go to B——, the place where I expected to lodge. They kept me waiting two hours before they came with the boat, consequently it was late when I got over. They were drunk and very profane, charged me four prices, and cursed me for troubling them. I gave them some tracts, and the best advice I could.

Soon after I met two women: one seemed

to be about thirty, and the other sixty years old. I offered them some tracts, which they at first declined, for fear I might be the sheriff. Neither knew a letter, or could tell who was the Saviour of sinners.

Soon after I passed them a terrible rain came on, and the roads were so deep my horse could scarcely draw my buggy. I saw night would soon overtake me, and the prospect of lodging looked unfavorable. I stopped at a cabin by the roadside to inquire the way, and leave some tracts. A man came out who looked as if he was ready for any crime, and came right up to my buggy, and began to look in with a scrutinizing eye. He eithe could not or would not give me any satisfac tion about the road. After an earnest exhortation about his soul, I gave him Baxter's Call. All the conduct of the man was of a very suspicious character.

It was now late, and raining hard, and in a little time would be very dark. I drove on as fast as possible, until it began to get quite dark, when I met a man on the road walking; whether he was a white man or not, I could not tell. I stopped him to inquire if there was any place near where I could lodge. He immediately began to examine the inside of my buggy as fully as the darkness would permit. He told me there was a man on the other bank of the creek, about half a mile ahead of me, who kept lodgers, and that it was a good place to stop. I handed him a book and thanked him, and drove on, he following a short distance, asking me questions which were not calculated to allay my anxiety.

I soon reached the creek, which seemed to be very high and rapid, and it was so dark I could see no object on the other side of it. The road entered by a narrow ravine, and there was no way to back out. I lifted my heart to God for protection, and drove in. In a moment the water was up in my buggy, but thanks to God, I got through safely, and in a few moments my horse was standing by the door of a miserable cabin.

I called, and a man came out with a torch of pine-knots in his hand. He was both dirty and ragged. I asked him where the man lived that kept lodgers. "Oh," said he, "I am the man that keeps tavern here." My prospects were bad, but I could get no further. I asked him to put up my tired horse and feed him. He had no stable but a rail-pen, no feed but some sheaves of green wheat. He took me to another cabin about fifty yards distant, that was as dark as a dungeon, except so far as his torch gave us light. Although it was warm, I requested him to make me a fire, which he did with reluctance.

After some time I was invited to the first cabin to supper. The man and his wife and children, as well as the supper, were all dirty in the extreme. I attempted to eat, but in vain. As soon as the man finished his meal, we returned to the other cabin, where I conversed with him. He was a total stranger to the simplest truths of the Bible.

I asked him if he knew any thing of the celebrated Lucas family of that county. "Oh yes," said he, "they live all round here. Did you not meet a man as you came along to-night about the top of the hill over the creek?" I said yes. "Well, that was one of them, and I wonder they let you pass so late in the evening. That one, and the one that lived in the house you last passed were the two implicated in killing the man for which one of their uncles was hung at Giles court-house, and if I had given in my testimony, they would have been hung too; and I am afraid they will kill me, because I know all about it."

By this time I was considerably alarmed. The conclusion I came to was that they were all linked together, and that I was in the slaughter-house.

I then inquired all about old Randal Lucas, who was the father of two that had been hung, and some others that were in prison, and was the grandfather of the two he had just been telling me about. He gave me a full history of the old man, much of which cannot be told. "But," said he, "such a man you never saw. He is ninety years old. When he puts on a suit of clothes, he never takes it off till it is worn out. In the winter he lies in the ashes, and in the summer he lies down in the mire like a hog." This is confirmed in Howe's History of Virginia, which relates how he sat under the gallows eating gingerbread while his sons were hung. I refer the reader to that history for an account of this wonderful man and his family.

The manner in which he told the whole story was any thing but pleasant to me. He began to get sleepy, and told me he would hold the pine-light while I got into bed up on the *loft*, as he called it. The only way to get up was by a ladder made of a pole split in two, with rounds put into it. I climbed up, and he followed me with the torch. As soon as I got to the bed over the loose boards that covered the floor, and found an old split-bottom chair, which I expected to use in self-defence before morning, I told him to withdraw.

I lay down without undressing, after committing my soul, family, and all my interests to God, without much hope of seeing the light of another day. No one occupied the house but myself as a bedroom. I kept watch till morning, and when any unpleasant sound was heard, I made noise enough to let any one approaching know that I was awake.

As soon as it was light I was up to see to my poor horse, which was standing in mud and water six inches deep, without food. After getting him some more green wheat in the sheaf, and a little corn bread for myself, and talking and praying with the family, I left them. I cannot say whether there was any intention to rob me or take my life. I hope there was not.

When I was about two miles on my way, and was rising a mountain where the road was scarcely six inches wider than my buggy, a man met me, riding a poor old horse without a saddle, all in rags and dirt, with nothing on him but remnants of a torn shirt and pants, with a rope tied round his waist, and a bottle of whiskey in his bosom. Such a looking piece of humanity I had never seen before. In a moment I concluded this is certainly old Randal Lucas. I saw he could not pass me on that narrow road, and I determined to have a full talk with him. When we met he tried to keep the upper side of the road, and get between my horse and the steep bank.

"Good morning, sir," said I. "Good morning," said he, in a very unnatural tone of voice. "Do n't you want some good books to read this morning?" "No, I do n't want any; I can't read." "Do you go to church?" "No, I do n't care about church." "Well, sir," said I, "you are an old man and must soon go to the other world." "Yes, I am ninety years old." "Is it possible," said I, "you are so old?" "Yes, I can prove it." "You would find but few witnesses to prove that by." "Well, I can swear it then." "Well, sir," said I, "what do you think will become of you when you die?" "O well, I *does'nt* care any thing about that." "Can you tell me who is the Saviour of sinners?" "I do n't know any thing of *them* things." "Well, sir, who made you?" "Why, I suppose it was God Almighty." "What is your name, sir?" "Randal Lucas." "Well," said I, "I thought so," straightening myself with a determined look. "Well, sir, you say you do n't go to church, and I must tell you in the name of my Master, that if you do n't repent you will soon be in hell. I have read and heard of you, sir, for years, and you stand on the brink of eternal burnings, and your soul stained with every crime that a man could commit." He began to look frightened, and tried to pass me; but I kept my position, and for some minutes laid down the terrors of the law in the strongest language

I could use, and then gave him some little books and tracts. He trembled like an aspen leaf.

A few weeks afterwards he took up the idea that he was soon to die, got a coffin made, tried it to see if it would fit, paid for it, and set it up in his cabin—sent for a preacher, told him he was going to die and did not know what would become of him, and asked him to pray for him; offered him fifty cents, and said, "Pray on till my money is done." The money was of course refused. In a few days the poor wretch died as he had lived, leaving a host of children the descendants of unnatural and brutal connection.

CHAPTER XIV.

TRAVELLING in a mountainous region at nightfall of a tempestuous day, and having lost my road, I was directed for a lodging to "Squire D——'s, who keeps the ferry." After supper, I had a pleasant talk with the father of Squire D——, on whose head the snows of eighty winters had fallen, and soon the family were gathered round us, engaged in delightful converse. I inquired as to the high-handed wickedness of a neighborhood not far off, where I had heard that meetings were frequently held in mockery of religious worship:

"Yes, yes," said the squire, with just enough of the Welsh accent to betray his origin, "and our neighborhood here was just as bad ten years ago; we were all alike: no church, no preacher, no Sunday-school, no day-school. One evening a minister and a young lady stopped at my house for the night; I thought them very inquisitive people. They asked if we had any preaching.

'No.' Any schools? 'No; we have had several teachers, but no one will stay more than a quarter with us.' The young lady said she would come and take a school among us, if we would employ her. After some further conversation, I told her I would see what could be done, and write her the result. Next morning they left for the minister's home at M——, some fifty miles distant.

"In a short time I had a school made up and board engaged for the new teacher, and wrote her to that effect She came and commenced her school at the time appointed. But soon there was complaint that the new teacher *read the Bible and prayed in her school.* And her troubles did not cease here. The man at whose house she boarded insisted that she should leave, because she prayed, sung hymns, and would keep talking about religion all the time. Miss H—— then set out to look up another home for herself; but she met the same reply from all: 'We cannot receive you unless you leave off praying and singing.'

"When she applied to me, I objected on the same grounds. Finally, I told her if she would come on my own terms, I would take her into my family. She inquired what those terms were. 'Why,' said I, 'you shall have such a room to yourself; there you are to stay from the time you return from school until you start to go back, only when you come to your meals: you must not sing hymns; you may pray as much as you please, but mind you do n't let us hear you at it; and *remember*, the first time you infringe this contract, you leave the premises.' To all this she agreed, with as much meekness as if my terms had been reasonable and right. That evening she took up her abode under my roof; and little did I think what a blessing God was sending me in that frail, delicate girl.

"The children all loved the new teacher very much. So one day she told them to ask their parents' permission, and if *they* were agreed, she would teach them on Sunday too. This proposal pleased us all. If she taught on Sunday, that was so much clear gain to us.

"I soon observed that my children took to staying in the teacher's room much of their time. At length, one Sunday morning, they came down with some tracts; I looked over them, and found they were on the subject of religion. Ah, said I, my lady, I 've caught you now. I called her down, told her she had violated her contract, and must be off. The poor girl began to weep; I felt ashamed. 'Dear sir,' said she, 'will you read those tracts? If you do, and still continue in your present mind, I will leave your house immediately.'

"Here was a pretty fix; the children were all crying, and begging me not to send Miss H—— away; and the books, Oh, they could not part with the books. I was mightily perplexed; at last I gave in. Said I, 'Miss H——, you may go back to your room; I will consider the matter.' I shall never forget the smile that passed over her face as she thanked me and went back to her room. Thanked me, indeed! Well, I set to work, read one of the tracts, felt self-condemned; read it again, felt dreadfully troubled. Then I read them all, and felt that I was a great sinner. I said nothing more to Miss H—— about leaving my house. Each day my convictions became deeper. At last, I could bear it no longer. Thought I, this wont do; I must talk with Miss H——. So I invited her to come and sit with us in the family. She cheerfully complied. I asked her a great many questions about the doctrines of the Bible, not meaning to let her know any thing about my concern. But all would not do; my distress continued, or rather my agony, for I thought I was the greatest sinner on earth.

"At last, I sent one evening for Miss H—— to come down, and I told her my troubles; for my proud heart was well-nigh broken. Said I, Miss H——, I feel so and so ever since I read those tracts of yours; and I related all that was passing in my mind; and, said I, do you think there is any mercy or hope for such a poor miserable sinner? The tears began to run down her cheeks; then she laughed; then she caught me by both hands, and looking up into my face, she said, 'Oh, my dear friend, I am *so* glad. 'Why,' said I, 'are you glad because I am in trouble?' 'Oh, my dear sir,' says she, 'this is the Spirit of God operating on your heart.' All at once a great light seemed to shine into my mind. All that I had been learning for so many weeks seemed now just as plain as A B C. Said I, 'Come, Miss H——, kneel down then and pray for me;' and she did pray for me, and I do bless God for his wonderful mercy to such a poor hardened sinner. I believe that God *did* change my heart just while that *very prayer* was going up. All at once it just came: I loved my Bible and I loved to pray, and I could not bear the company that I used to take so much delight in.

"On the next Sabbath, Miss H—— asked me to go along with her and the children to the school—which was, and had been a Sunday-school, though we never suspected it; and here came a trial. If I go, they will say I am getting religious; if I stay, it will be a sin, for I know I *ought* to go; and then it will grieve Miss H——. These last considerations were the strongest; so I went. The room was crowded with children, all waiting for their teacher; I thought they all looked happy. After a little while, Miss H—— took the Bible, and coming to me, she said, 'Mr. D——, will you read and pray with us this morning?' I was startled; my very heart trembled. Said I, 'Oh no; not now.' Then she read a chapter and prayed herself. Oh, how I felt, to think that I was ashamed to pray before those children! Ah, thought I, this will never do; I will come here and pray next Sunday. That night I read and prayed with my family; and the next Sabbath I opened the school with prayer.

"The news spread soon all through the settlement. D—— has got religion and is praying in the Sunday-school! strange news this! Very soon the people began to drop into our Sunday-school. Then Miss H—— said to me, 'You had better read us a sermon at the Sunday-school, after the other exercises are over.' She selected the sermons, and I read them. Our meetings grew very solemn. Presently we sent word to a good man at B—— to send us a minister; he did so. The minister came and preached for us. The little school-house could not contain one half of the people who crowded to hear him. We held our meetings in the open air, under the trees.

"Ah, that was a wonderful time; the cry

of the anxious sinner went up from every house. The Spirit of God was moving mightily upon the hearts of the people, and many were born into the kingdom of Christ. All this brought a great change in our settlement. Instead of the dance, and the gaming-table, and the foolish song, we had meetings for prayer and praise; and the tavern and still-house were exchanged for the temple of God.

"The Sabbath became a day of holy rest among a people who used to spend it in revelry or idleness. Houses of worship were built, where our population flocked every Sabbath to hear the preached word from the living minister; and in the course of two or three years, hundreds professed faith in Christ, and joined the church. We have had a flourishing church here ever since. Ah," said the good man, in his peculiarly emphatic way, "see what God hath wrought for us."

How often have I reproached myself, when I contrasted the heroic conduct of this devoted female with my own man-fearing spirit! She has gone to her reward; her memory will be cherished for a few more years in the hearts of those to whom her humble efforts were of such immense value, and then pass away and be forgotten. But her *influence* will pass on, an ever-increasing current, down the long tracts of time, and throughout the endless ages of eternity.

CHAPTER XV.

THE latter part of the year 1848 was spent laboring in South-western Virginia. I visited several towns as a colporteur, taking with me some applicant for this service, to give him a favorable introduction to his labors.

I reached the beautiful town of A—— late in the evening, an entire stranger, and stopped at a hotel, wet, cold, and hungry. About the same time the stage arrived with a number of passengers, and we all asked for rooms with fire in them. While this was preparing I stepped into the bar-room, the only place where I could find a fire; but it had been election day, and such a company of intoxicated men I had never seen in one room. Several of them were lying on the floor, unable to rise; and the swearing was awful. I immediately began the distribution of tracts and little paper-covered books; and among them I laid down a copy of "Universalism not of God." As I passed round, laying them down on chairs and tables, as well as handing them to the men, I observed a very fine-looking man who had come in the stage, following me, and looking at them.

As I laid down "Universalism not of God," he took it up, and said to me very abruptly that the book was a libel on the Universalists. "Oh," said I, "I understand the cause of your objection to the book. You are one of those who believe that thieves, murderers, and liars all go to heaven; that there is no such place as hell." "Yes," said he, "I have too good an opinion of God's mercy to believe there is any such place as hell." When he made that remark, one of the fellows who was lying drunk on the floor raised his head and said, "You are a liar;" while another said he "wished that was true, but there was no such good news." Said I, "Sir, I will hand you over to these men, and you and they may settle the controversy." He immediately disappeared from the room.

During my stay of three weeks in this beautiful town, I visited every family in it, and either sold or gave books.

One day I stepped into the office of a lawyer, who was one of the first men in the state in his profession. I offered him a copy of Nelson on Infidelity. Said he, "I could not take time to read a book of that size, except on law, for less than five hundred dollars." I then offered him Baxter's Call. Said he, "That is too big a dose for me too." I then presented him the tract, "The Great Alternative." "Well," said he, "as you are so anxious for me to read some of your books, I will read that right off." He commenced, and I left him. An hour or two after I was passing his door, and he was sitting in a thoughtful mood. Said I, "Have you read the tract?" "Yes," said he, "and if I would read a few more like it I think I might become a Christian." Said I, "Too busy to be saved." "Yes," said he, "I fear that is my case; I have not a moment to spare from my business." Alas, how many will have to say, I was too busy to be saved.

In the same town there was a man who had once been a minister of some prominence in an evangelical church, but had left it, and embraced the doctrines of Swedenborg, for which he was very zealous. I did not wish to encounter him; but as I stepped into a store one night to scatter tracts, he was present. He immediately made an attack on me, and said that he could not imagine how any wise man could believe in the doctrine of the Trinity; that it was so absurd that nothing in heaven or earth could illustrate it. I saw the eyes of all present were turned to me, and felt in a tight place. I lifted my heart to God for help to vindicate his truth. A candle was burning between us. Said I, pointing to the candle, "Sir, there is a trinity giving us light. There is tallow, wick, and fire, three in one." He acknowledged he was beat, and took his leave, to the amusement of those present, and to my great satisfaction.

After two months' labor in South-western Virginia, I returned to my home in L——, near two hundred miles distant from A——, and devoted a month to correspondence and adjusting accounts with over fifty colporteurs I had now employed.

Though L—— had been my home for over two years, I had never had time to visit all the families with our books and tracts. I had often determined to do it, but other labors had prevented. The number of warm friends and liberal contributors in and around the town seemed to lay special claims on me to do the work, and I resolved to spend the months of January and February laboring in the town and vicinity.

At this time it was remarked by the ministers and praying people of God, that they had not felt such a spiritual dearth there for many years. The ball-room was better attended than the churches, and the young seemed to be rushing into sin with greediness. My own soul too was in darkness, and my strength nearly prostrated. My devotions, public and private, were heartless. I was even tempted to leave my work and engage in some secular business.

At last I told a few of the most pious whom I knew about the desire I had to visit the families, and that the state of my own heart was such that I was prevented from doing it. They urged me forward, and promised to pray for me. I set day after day to begin; but when the day and hour came for me to start, my heart would fail, and Satan seemed to have some excuse always ready. At last I entered into covenant with God to begin the next day; but when the morning came my hard, cowardly heart failed me. I tried to pray again and again. I put it off till the afternoon, with a hope of getting strength. A carpet-bag had been standing full of books and tracts for some days waiting, and they seemed to rebuke my cowardice.

At last I thought that if Moses had not stepped into the Red sea, the waters would never have receded. The next morning still found me at home. As soon as my breakfast was over I took the carpet-bag and books to a room and earnestly prayed over them, and then started.

The next neighbor to me was a Mr. H——. His wife and mother-in-law were devoted Christians, but he was careless about religion, and so was his brother, a young man that had his home there. I dealt faithfully with them, and prayed with them. Each of them bought a book, and I left them in tears. Soon after the young man professed religion, and the other remained serious as long as I knew him. All my fears were now gone. A few minutes before I was ashamed to own Christ before a kitchen-maid; now I could face the world, and the promise was realized, "My strength is made perfect in weakness."

I next went to Mr. P——'s and had a long talk with his daughter, a very intelligent girl of twelve summers. In a short time she professed religion.

I next entered the house of Mr. R——. He and his wife were two of the friends to whom I had told my difficulties, and who had engaged to pray for me. They had two very interesting daughters that moved in the most fashionable circles of society. As soon as I entered the house they knew my errand. I was directed to the parlor, and told by the father, "I will send the girls in, and wife and I will go into our own room and pray while you talk." I felt God was there while I talked and prayed. One received Pike's Persuasives to Early Piety, the reading of which led her to the Saviour soon after; the other got Baxter's Call, and was an inquirer during all the time I remained there.

I cannot find words to express the joy I felt in my own soul at the close of this day's work. All nature seemed to rejoice with me, and I fully realized the promise, "He that watereth shall be watered."

The next day I visited eleven families, talked and prayed and sold and gave books and tracts in every house. In almost every house some feeling was manifested, and soon after several professed religion. Among them was a Mrs. M——, who told me it was the Anxious Inquirer that led her to Christ. I visited half the town in a week, and sold and gave away many books and tracts. Quite a number of those visited showed much feeling while I talked with them.

At this time special religious services were held in one of the churches that had but little sympathy at that time with the Tract Society, or any thing else that was not under their own exclusive control; and I was advised to stop my work till their meeting closed, for fear they might say I was proselyting. I attended all their meetings, and prayed and exhorted when called on. Their meetings continued two weeks, during which time twenty professed religion, most of whom I had previously visited.

At the close of these meetings, I told the

Rev. Dr. McE—— that now was the time for him to have meetings in his church. He said he was not able to do any extra work, and did not know where he could get any preacher. I proposed to get the Rev. R. N. D——, who was then laboring as a colporteur of the Tract Society some fifty miles distant, to which he agreed, and I wrote to Mr. D—— to come on a certain day. During the intervening time of ten days I visited all the balance of the town and held prayer-meetings every night. The meetings became more and more interesting, and religion became the theme of conversation in every circle.

When Mr. D—— came public preaching was held every night, and the word was attended with the power of God. Every morning we had a prayer-meeting, and through the day visited the inquirers from house to house, and scattered tracts. By the end of four days thirty-five were attending the meeting for inquiry, and at the close of the first week thirty-three had professed hope in Christ, most of them the most influential people in the town.

The Rev. Mr. V—— then came and aided

another week, at the close of which forty-two were added to the church. Thus did God carry on his work with the humble instruments he had chosen.

One young lady who had been an inquirer .or two weeks, told us at last she did not care about being converted then, and left the meetings. In three weeks she died. Her last words were, "I could have been saved, but I rejected God's Spirit, and now I am lost."

Another came sometimes to the inquiry meetings, but owing to the fact that she was soon to marry an irreligious man, put off her day of grace. In a few weeks the day of her intended marriage came. She rose in the morning in usual health to prepare for the ceremony, but before night her costly bridal dress was her winding-sheet.

Four miles from town Mr. W——, a colporteur, was at work during the time of this meeting in the town, and ten were there added to a little church.

I have been thus particular in stating the facts in relation to this work, as it was the starting point of one of the most powerful revivals that I have ever witnessed. It extended over one hundred miles square of a sparsely populated country, in which near one thousand souls were converted to God within about four months. The fidelity and perseverance in the service of Christ of those thus brought in, is the best evidence that this was truly the work of God's Spirit.

At the close of these cheering labors in L—, I went to the town of U—— to be with Mr. H—— at a sacramental meeting, and take a collection for the Tract Society. He is one of God's ministers that does his work faithfully. The meeting began on Friday night. Mr. H—— requested me to occupy the time in giving an account of the great work at L——, which I did. Although but few were present, and they mostly pupils in the academy he taught, the bare relation of the facts of the revival at L—— made a deep impression, and resulted in the conversion of his son, who is now a minister.

The next morning at nine, we had a meeting for prayer and exhortation, at which there was still more interest. At eleven Mr. H—— preached. At night I conducted the service by exhortation and prayer. The solemnity was still increased. At each meeting we gave each one present a suitable tract, with a word of earnest counsel.

At nine, Sabbath morning, I conducted another prayer-meeting. At eleven, Mr. H—— preached and administered the communion. God was truly there in great power. At three we had a meeting for prayer again. At night the church was full. I based my remarks on the words, "I will arise and go to my father." I saw that every heart was moved, and but few cheeks were dry. At the close of my remarks, I turned to Mr. H——, and said to him, "If you will ask them, some anxious souls will remain for instruction and prayer." The result was, seven inquirers took a stand on the Lord's side that night. This seemed to rouse the great soul of Mr. H—— to an extraordinary pitch of fervor, and led to the appointment of a meeting the next morning.

On Monday morning we both exhorted, and the interest was deep. At three we held an inquiry-meeting, and nine attended. At night I spoke again; the meeting was deeply interesting.

Tuesday morning the prayer-meeting was crowded, and in the afternoon there were seventeen inquirers. We had three services each day, the one at three only for inquirers; and each day there was an increase of interest. On Saturday morning Mr. H—— had to go some miles to another preaching-place, and I was left alone on Saturday and the Sabbath. Sabbath, at three, there were twenty-seven inquirers, and ten were indulging a hope in Christ. During the next week forty-two professed faith in Christ.

In the whole course of these meetings we kept the very choicest of our books and tracts in the hands of the people. One observing Christian said to me, "There has been more reading here on the subject of religion in the past eighteen days, than there had been in three years before." Quite a number of the inquirers told me they were first awakened by reading a book or tract, and others that they were greatly aided by them in coming to Christ. Their interest in these publications was shown by their contributing one hundred dollars on one of the Sabbaths to aid the tract and colporteur work.

This town was one of the wickedest in Western Virginia, and had for years been a centre of infidelity. A worthy farmer who lived near told me, at the close of our meetings, that for years he had never passed through that town without hearing oaths and vulgar songs; "but now," said he, "that is all stopped, and I hear them singing hymns of praise to God." This town will now compare favorably with any other within my knowledge for piety and sobriety.

CHAPTER XVI.

At the earnest request of Mr. H——, I promised to meet him on the next Sabbath at one of his country churches, about six miles from town, in one of the most densely populated and wealthy communities in all Western Virginia, called Mount P——. It was only fourteen miles from my home at L——. I reached the church a little before the hour of service, a stranger to all except a few who had met me at the meetings in town. The house, although large, was crowded, and I took a seat in the back part of the house. In a few minutes Mr. H—— came in and walked up into the pulpit. He looked sick and feeble, and while glancing his eye over the house, saw me, and beckoned me to him. He was unable to speak louder than a whisper.

Said he, "I am attacked with bronchitis and unable to preach, and you must preach." This I refused, on the ground that I had no authority. Said he, "I will give you the authority here, and stand between you and danger." He arose, and with great exertion told the people that he had never had such a desire to preach as he had that day, but the Lord had shut his mouth, and sent me to do the preaching, for which he was very thankful.

I at once opened with singing and prayer, and announced my text, "Behold, I stand at the door and knock." I felt that the thoughts and words were not mine, but dictated by the Holy Ghost. I spoke for an hour. The audience was still as the grave. After an interval of thirty minutes, as was the custom, we resumed the service. My text in the afternoon was, "Remember now thy Creator in the days of thy youth." The feeling was deep. I asked the anxious to remain for instruction, and twelve remained. At night I had a meeting at a private house, where great interest was manifested.

At the earnest request of many, services similar to those of the Sabbath were continued on Monday and for several days afterwards. On Monday morning, when I came to the church, there was a crowd, and much to my joy and relief, Mr. W——, one of our best colporteurs, was there. He had labored faithfully over all that ground but a few weeks before, and knew almost every one in that region. Although very diffident, he conducted the morning meeting with great acceptance. I spoke at eleven, and at two; and at the close of the last service we had eighteen inquirers. God seemed to come down as on the day of Pentecost. Ten of the number indulged hope, and their countenances were lit up with joy.

At night we had a meeting at Mr. D——'s. One half could not get into the house. He had a son that was desperately wicked, and had done all in his power to oppose the work of God. During the time of the service he went out of the house in an agony of conviction for sin. The next morning, at family prayers, he cried out in the bitterness of his anguish, "God be merciful to me a sinner." A sister of his, that had been a very thoughtless girl, also cried out in great distress. This seemed instantly to electrify the whole family. The place seemed awful with the majesty of God. I felt as much of the divine glory as I could bear. Such a scene I had never witnessed. Soon the whole family were embraced in each other's arms, rejoicing in hope of eternal life. We seemed to be in the inner sanctuary and the most holy place. Although near fourteen years have since passed, while I describe this scene it fires my own soul afresh.

Though it was a hurried season of the year with farmers, work was suspended, ploughs were stopped, white and black were in the church, or as near in as they could get, as the church would not hold more than half that came.

The Tuesday morning prayer-meeting was one of the best I ever attended. At eleven the Rev. Mr. H—— returned, and preached one of the best of sermons. In the afternoon I spoke again. There were thirty-six more inquirers, and twelve more were indulging hope.

On Friday night I held a meeting at the house of a Dr. N——, who was a man of the world. I spoke on the *broad road and wide gate.* The doctor was awakened that night and has ever since dated his first impressions on religious subjects to that time; and two young men, one of them since educated for the ministry, likewise dated their conversion the same night.

At eleven the next morning Rev. Mr. H—— preached, and in the afternoon Dr. McE——. At the close of this service, sixty-two were added to the church on profession of their faith.

When the hour for public worship arrived on Sabbath morning, one half could not enter the church. It was arranged that I should invite those who could not get in to assemble out of hearing of the church and preach to them. I selected the graveyard, where most of the graves had enclosures of rails around and over them. The circumstance suggested my text: "Man dieth, and wasteth away; yea, man giveth up the ghost, and where is he?" I felt as I never did before, standing among the dead and the living, and spoke as I never did before or since. Some of the wickedest men in all the country were before me.

One gray-headed sinner seventy years old, who sat on the rails which were around the graves of his wife and children, shook as if he had the ague. A year after, he died; and often, when he was on his death-bed, spoke with deep sorrow of resisting God's Spirit at that time. At the close of the services in the church a collection of $120 was taken up for the Tract Society, which was five times as much as could have been obtained a week before. Books and tracts were circulated every day in these meetings, and read with interest. Twenty persons told me that books or tracts were the means of either awakening them, or directing them to Christ. In addition to the sixty-two added to the church as above, twenty-four who obtained a hope at these meetings joined a church of another denomination a mile distant.

Only two miles from the above meetings, was the church of a large congregation of Seceders. Till this time they had not gone to hear any preacher but their own, nor admitted any other denomination to preach in their church. But so great was this work that some of their young people had been drawn away, and gained a hope in Christ, but kept it secret. Their pastor, Rev. Mr. McG——, came himself on Saturday, and became deeply moved with what he saw and heard. In the evening Rev. Mr. H—— told him there were many still anxious about their souls, and not a few of them were among his own people; "and now," said he, "this harvest must be gathered, and if you will go on with a meeting next week I will close my meetings to-morrow." This arrangement was made, and it was agreed that I should go and assist Mr. McG—— on the afternoon of the next day, after the services in that church should be closed.

At four o'clock the Seceder church was crowded, and all the ardor of feeling seemed to come along with the people. Rev. Mr. McG—— was very feeble in health, but was a devoted servant of God; and it was arranged that he was to take a text and speak ten minutes, and I was then to fill up the hour. After that service we held another in a private house at night.

The next morning at nine, we had the house full at the prayer-meeting. At eleven, Mr. McG—— preached ten minutes, and I followed; and after the service all were supplied with tracts. During the afternoon service the presence of God seemed to move every heart. And as I believe that when God moves on men's hearts, they ought to move too as the prodigal did, when I had ceased speaking, and the congregation were singing the eighty-fourth Psalm, Rouse's version, I said to Mr. McG—— that I had no doubt but if an invitation was given some would remain for instruction. He feared it would not be acceptable to the officers of the church, all of whom had come from Scotland, and had been accustomed to hear preaching only from Seceders, and considered *occasional hearing* an offence. But he said he would not interfere with what I thought was duty.

As soon as the song was sung, I arose and told them that a piece of old Scotch history had just come into my mind. That over one hundred years ago, previous to their communion occasions, the minister at the close of his services for some days would invite all that intended to commune for the first time to remain for instruction in regard to their duties; and that for want of that many came to the Lord's table who were ignorant of the nature of the ordinance. And as I believed there were a number who contemplated joining the church and going to the communion table on the next Sabbath for the first time, I would ask all such to remain after the congregation was dismissed, to receive such instruction as should be given. After some agitation all was quiet, and I told them the first point of inquiry for them was, to know if they were born again, and spoke some twenty minutes on the nature and evidences of regeneration. The old elders sobbed aloud; and as soon as the services were closed, they had me by the hand, and said, "That is just what our young people need." The oldest elder, whose daughter was among the inquirers, came up leaning on his staff, and said, "That did my soul good." We had an appointment that night five miles distant, and this old man went all the way with me on horseback. The house was crowded. Many were awakened, and among them Mr. B—— the proprietor, who was a hardened sinner of fifty years. He soon professed his faith in Christ.

The next morning this old elder, Mr. M——, said to me, "Oh, Mr. C——, I slept none last night. I have had a foretaste of heaven, and long to be there. I have never experienced religious joy till last night; and now I have one request to make, and deny me not, that is, that you commune with me next Sabbath."

The next day we had similar services, and at the close of the last service I told them as all the congregation seemed desirous to hear what was said to those wishing to consider their duty to join the church, such would come forward while we sung the twenty-third Psalm. Sixteen thus presented themselves, and Rev. Mr. McG—— spoke to them with a heavenly unction. The next day there were twenty-eight inquirers, and the next day thirty-nine, of whom twenty-two appeared to be indulging a good hope in Christ. All the business of the field was suspended, and many were saying it was the dawn of the day of glory to the church. As the time had arrived for me to visit another place fifty miles distant, to engage in similar labors, the pastor told them he wanted them to make a thank-offering to the Tract Society, and in a few minutes $80 was on the table, and a present of $20 to me. On the Sabbath fifty-six were added to the church, and more than thirty to a Methodist church near by.

Fourteen months after, I visited this church again. The presence of God was still there, and many said they felt as if they were ready to begin again where they had left off fourteen months before. The strong prejudices against worshipping with other Christians were among the things that had been.

During my brief stay many incidents were related to me. One young man told me it was "Advice to a Married Couple" that awakened him, as he was soon to be married. Three of the anxious got relief by reading the tract "What is it to Believe in Christ?" A man well acquainted in the community told me thirty family altars were reared on one Sabbath night.

In one instance two families lived in one house, and both the men and their wives had joined the church. They felt that they must have family worship, but neither was willing to pray. One said he could do the singing, and the other said he would read the Bible. At last they united in asking a lame negro man that was pious, and he led in prayer.

There is probably no region of our country, when all the difficulties are considered, where the Tract Society and colporteurs have done as much real good as in Western Virginia. Some of the most godly men we ever employed had visited every house again and again, and most of the books to be found in the houses were the Society's publications. In some of the poorer districts they were even the only school-books. I have heard of schools in those mountains where one had Bunyan, another Baxter's Call, or Saints' Rest, and so on all through the school. We can say that in many places the work has made the wilderness and the solitary place rejoice and blossom as the rose.

CHAPTER XVII.

After one night's rest at home, I left the next morning for C——, thirty miles distant, to meet my friend Rev. Mr. D——, who was with us at the commencement of the meetings at L——, and engage in another meeting. The Rev. Mr. P——, who was pastor at that place, was likewise a colporteur of the Tract Society, and had five little churches in as many different communities in the county. So he left us to hold a meeting in C——, while he was laboring in other portions of his field.

I had on several occasions passed through this town, which, in a religious view, was one of the darkest I have ever visited. I saw the men, most of them young men, while Mr. P—— was preaching to a few, mostly women, standing all round the church with their heads in the windows, talking aloud, and even swearing profanely, till the preacher's voice could scarcely be heard. As Mr. D—— was a stranger there, I informed him that we might expect open opposition. The meetings were to be conducted in the same way as those to which I have already alluded.

After warning the people of the impropriety of such conduct, and insisting that if they attended the services, they should come into the church, Mr. D—— preached, and I followed by telling of the Lord's work in the places where I had been. A deep solemnity seemed to fall on every soul, and we felt God was there. All present were well supplied with tracts.

The next day our meetings were very solemn, and still more so at night, when there were five anxiously inquiring for salvation. By the next night most of the females began to feel very deeply, and some young men began to interrupt by their talking; but I rebuked them most solemnly, and we had no more interruptions during that meeting, and I am happy to say there have been none since in that place.

This meeting began on Thursday night, and by Monday twenty-two had professed hope in Christ. Among the number was one man sixty years old. He had been intemperate forty years. Though he was then so ignorant that he did not know who was the Saviour of sinners, and did not know one letter of the alphabet, he still lives a monument of grace.

One young lady of fortune, who was there at school, and whose anxiety about her soul bordered on despair, gained a hope on Saturday. On the next Saturday she joined the church, and then told her companions, "I will go to the Lord's table to-morrow; it may be my last Sabbath on earth." On Monday morning she came to school apparently in her usual health, and seemed deeply affected by the opening prayer; but soon complained of being unwell, went to her boarding-house, and in forty-eight hours she was numbered with the dead. Grace and glory came very near together.

After a few days of rest, at the request of the Rev. Mr. H——, to whom I have alluded at the town of U——, I met him in an old log-church on Wolf Creek, one of his preaching-places. I left home in the morning, rode twenty-four miles, and reached the place at one. Mr. H—— was preaching to a small congregation, as it was now the beginning of harvest. After an interval of thirty minutes, I addressed the people. The next day was Saturday. The house was full; and in the evening we had five inquirers. Sabbath morning Mr. H—— preached with great power, and then left for another appointment, with the expectation of returning on Monday. In the mean time I was to go on with the services. In the evening I had thirteen inquirers; and among them was Colonel H——, fifty years old, and Major B——, sixty-eight, two men of the largest wealth and highest standing in that community, who had been remarkable instances of grieving the Spirit of God. I related in their hearing the fact of what an aged man had told me about his grieving the Spirit. I saw it affected them both very deeply. They told me they had felt all that that man did whose case I had described, and that they had now made up their minds to seek Christ. In a few days both were hoping in Christ; and two years ago they had continued active Christians.

Becoming exhausted, almost as if I was at

death's door, I left for home; but Rev. Mr. H—— continued the meetings. Such was the interest awakened, that daily labor in the harvest-field was entirely suspended. Masters and servants were all at the same mercy-seat. God was there; the world was lost sight of, and eternal things took its place. Everybody had a tract in hand. You could see them reading on their way home; some in carriages, some on horseback, and others on foot. The result was, thirty-six were added to that little church, and many others to the other churches in that region of country. I soon learned that one wild, thoughtless young woman was awakened by reading a tract, and she is now one of the mothers in Israel.

I had received several letters from the Rev. Mr. C——, an aged man who had moved to Fayette county, to preach in a very destitute region, near the celebrated *Hawk's Nest*, or *Marshall's Pillar*, a cliff or precipice of about one thousand feet perpendicular height, hanging over New River, ten miles from its junction with the Gauley. After a day of rest, I took the stage, and at the end of fifty miles reached the place. On Friday morning the meeting began in the woods. No church was near; but an arbor was made by putting up poles and covering them with green bushes. When I came it rained, and only about thirty were present; but God was there with his gracious power. We had a meeting in the evening at one of the neighboring cabins, and a crowd was collected.

The next morning we met at the arbor The day was fair and beautiful, and the crowd great. The Lord helped me greatly in the service. At the interval I scattered tracts freely, and set all to reading who could read. At the close of the afternoon service there were eleven anxious inquirers. On Sabbath morning we met at nine for prayer. By eleven o'clock a thousand people had assembled; and after the evening service, seventeen came out for instruction. On Monday the communion was to be administered, and seventeen were added to the Lord's people. The Lord was there in his mercy. After the afternoon service nineteen more came out as inquirers, among them men of sixty years and from that down to boys, most of whom professed religion soon after. A church was soon after organized, which still lives. The blessed influence spread for miles around, and all denominations shared in the glorious work. I shall ever believe the way was prepared by a faithful colporteur, who had been over the ground a few months before.

Mr. P——, an elder in a vacant church called Locust Bottom, had applied to the Rev. Mr. P—— to come and administer the communion in that church, and to bring me with him. The meeting was to begin on the Friday before the third Sabbath in August. I left home on Thursday morning, and reached the place, fifty-four miles distant, at noon the next day. In the afternoon I addressed the audience by telling them what the Lord had done in so many other places, and that I felt assured if they would seek him with their whole hearts he would bless them too.

The next morning we were assembled at nine for prayer and exhortation. At eleven Mr. C——, a student of divinity, spoke with much fervor. After recess I spoke with much liberty, and five came out as inquirers. We held meetings at night in two places; both well attended, and several were awakened.

The Sabbath morning prayer-meeting was crowded. The communion was administered by Mr. P—— ; and after recess I spoke again, and we had nine inquirers. The next morning we had a crowd, and there were clear indications of the presence of the Spirit of God.

Some weeks previous, Mr. W——, a colporteur to whom I have alluded, had been all through this region, and circulated books. A daughter of Colonel S——, one of the elders, became awakened by reading one of them, and her state of mind had aroused some of her friends and companions, who were among those most deeply concerned; and it was agreed to hold the evening meeting at the colonel's, though four miles distant.

In addition to the colonel's large family, a number of others were present, all seeking peace with God. After tea was over we were all seated in a large parlor, to the number of at least twenty. As Mr. C—— expected soon to leave, I asked him to lead us in prayer, and especially to remember the anxious souls in the room. At the close of the prayer, one of the colonel's daughters was sobbing as if she would break her heart. I sat down beside her, and pointed her to Jesus who died for sinners. She looked at me a moment, and then sprang into her mother's arms, and said, "Oh, mother, I have found Jesus." But a short time had elapsed, when a daughter-in-law of Mrs. S—— went to her and said, "Oh, mother, I have found the Saviour too." Soon the wife of one of the elders who was there cried, "Oh, Mrs. S——, the Saviour has blessed me too. Oh, what a Saviour I have found." This woman had been so opposed to religion that her husband could not have family prayers. All these three had been awakened by reading tracts. During all this time the old grandmother, ninety years old, and for over seventy years a follower of Christ, was walking through the house saying, "Oh, Mr. C——, is not this heaven? my poor soul can bear no more of the divine glory."

In a short time Colonel S——, who had been absent, returned. As soon as his daughter saw him she was in his arms, saying, "Oh, my dear father, your prayers are answered, I have found Jesus."

By this time the news had spread all over the farm, and more than fifty blacks of all ages were in and round the house. The old mother of Col. S—— said to me, "Oh, Mr. C——, wont you preach to these poor souls?" "Certainly," said I; and in a few minutes a large room was crowded with them. I stood in the door, with the old mother holding me by the arm, and announced the words, "Behold, I bring you glad tidings of great joy which shall be to all people." The negroes soon became so excited they could hardly contain themselves. Some were on their knees praying, and others clapping their hands. The old lady undertook to keep them in order; but her own heart became so deeply impressed, that her bodily strength sunk under it. The scene was one that neither tongue nor pen can describe. No doubt some who have never seen or felt any thing like this, will call it enthusiasm; but if it was, I would wish to live and die in the midst of such enthusiasm. This was one of the most intelligent families in that community—all educated and refined, and strict Presbyterians. I have found but few such families.

The next morning we all repaired to the church, where I was met by Mr. W——, the colporteur whom I have mentioned. Before that day's meeting closed eight more professed hope. That night I had a meeting at a Mr. C——'s, who was a professed atheist, but within a few days after, was numbered among God's people.

The next day the house was crowded below with whites, and the gallery with blacks. The presence of God seemed to be with every soul. There were in the house two men, brothers, of large wealth and much intelligence, both unmarried and somewhat dissipated. For two days they had been deeply concerned, and their pious friends were earnest in prayer for them. Just as I was closing my last discourse in the evening, when there was scarce a dry cheek in the house, a negro who was subject to fits, fell in a fit in the gallery, and made the most unearthly noise I ever heard. All fled from the house with fright, thinking the house was falling. These two brothers, when they went out, said they were glad at what had happened, for if they had remained any longer they would have been compelled to yield to the Spirit of God. They both went away, and never returned;

and said often afterwards that they sealed their damnation that day. Each of them died a horrible death with delirium tremens.

I exhorted three or four times each day throughout all the week, and brother W—— scattered books and tracts, and talked and prayed. Twenty-two were added to that church, and as many more joined other churches. Before this meeting began, that church was nearly broken up, and in six months after, the student to whom I have alluded was the pastor.

Ten years after, as I was passing through this region in a stage, one of my travelling companions told me he was one of the converts at a place where I had labored. We were alone in the stage when we reached the place of crossing a river near this church. The driver stopped to water his horses, and I handed tracts to two men that were working at the edge of the river. They looked at me a moment, and then caught my hands: "Oh, this is Mr. C——. It was your tracts and labors that God blessed to save our souls." The stage-driver dropped his bucket and rushed to me: "Oh, is it possible I have been hauling Mr. C—— and did not know it? It was your tracts and labors which you began in the rain in Fayette county that God blessed to my soul." Here were four men who had been led to Christ at different places, and now had met the one whom they called the instrument of their salvation. To God alone be all the glory.

CHAPTER XVIII.

As, in the providence of God, I have been brought into contact with thousands of persons who have told me with much candor the history of their own minds, and conversed freely in reference to the all-important subject of their salvation, I have thought it to be my duty to record some of the facts I have met, for the benefit and warning of others. That there is a point when the Holy Spirit, if wilfully and perseveringly resisted, ceases to strive with man, no one doubts who believes in his renewing and sanctifying agency; but too many take it for granted that this point is not reached till the close of life, and neglect or resist the strivings of the Spirit till he gives them up to hardness of heart and blindness of mind, perhaps many years before their earthly existence has terminated.

The first case I shall mention is that of a woman about thirty years of age, with whom I conversed in the presence of her mother. I inquired if she was a member of any church.

She answered, "No." I asked if she had not at some time felt concern for her salvation. "Yes," she said, "I think but few have been more anxious on the subject than I was once." I asked at what period of her life this occurred, when she gave me the following account of God's dealings with her. "When I was about fifteen years old, I felt that I was a great sinner in the sight of God. Often my distress was so great that I could not sleep; and for three years I seldom had peace for a week at a time. I knew that the Holy Spirit was striving with me, and that I ought to yield my heart to his influence; but I thought it would cut off my pleasures in the midst of youth. I tried to banish the thoughts of eternity; but they would still return and interrupt my pleasure. I tried reading novels and romances; they gave me relief for a while, but my distress returned. At last I went to the ballroom—and I have never since had such feelings as before." "And have you no fears," said I, "that you have grieved away the Spirit of God for ever?" "Yes," she replied, "I have no doubt of that, and that I shall be lost." I proceeded to describe the state and misery of the lost, and appealed to her, by the prayers of her mother and the tears which were then falling from her sunken eyes, by the danger of an eternal separation from pious friends, by the glories of heaven and the agonies of the Son of God, now to make her peace with him and be saved. "All this," she calmly replied, "has been tried upon me before. Nothing that you or any other man can say on that subject, can move me now. My doom is fixed."

Another case was that of Mr. B——, who was over seventy years old, and living an ungodly life. I approached him with kindness, and at length he conversed freely. I spoke of the goodness of God to him in his advanced years, and asked if he hoped he had an interest in Christ. He replied, "No." I asked if he received the Bible as the word of God. He answered, "Yes." I said, "The Bible teaches that a man must be born again before he can enter the kingdom of God; do you think you have experienced that change?" "No," said he, "I never have." I saw that he was intelligent, and inquired if no "still small voice" had ever whispered to him, "Son, give me thy heart?" "Yes," said he, "often. I used to feel, but for many years I have not felt as I did when I was young. I then had some very serious times." I asked at what period he had felt most deeply the importance of religion. He replied, "When I was seventeen I began to feel deeply at times, and this continued for two or three years; but I determined to put it off till I should be settled in life. After I was married, I reflected that the time had come when I had promised to attend to religion; but I had bought this farm, and I thought it would not suit me to become religious till it was paid for, as some time would have to be devoted to attend church, and also some expense. I then resolved to put it off ten years; but when the ten years came round, I thought no more about it. I often try to think, but I cannot keep my mind on the subject one moment." I urged him by all the terrors of dying an enemy of God, to set about the work of repentance. "It is too late," said he, "I believe my doom is sealed; and it is just that it should be so, for the Spirit strove long with me, but I refused." I then turned to his children, young men and young women who were around him, and entreated them not to put off the subject of religion, or grieve the Spirit of God in their youthful days. The old man added, "Mind *that*. If I had attended to it then, it would have been well with me today; but now it is too late."

On conversing with a man in middle life, he informed me that his father was a devoted Christian, that he was faithfully instructed and his mind was early impressed with the importance of religion. In his youth, there was a period of six months in which he was in distress, day and night; and a voice within seemed to be continually saying, "Forsake your sins and come unto me, and I will give you peace." "But," he added, "I did not wish to be a Christian then; I thought it would ruin my pleasures. I visited a part of the country where dancing and balls were frequent; in a little time my serious thoughts were gone, and I have never had any since." I asked if he did not fear that God had given him up. "Yes," said he, "I am afraid he has. I go to church and read the Bible, and try to feel, but I cannot." I strove to arouse his fears, but it was in vain. I afterwards learned that he was pursuing his worldly business on the Sabbath.

It is not for me to pronounce that God had said of all these persons, they are "joined to their idols, let them alone;" "woe to them when I depart from them;" but the state of all such is unspeakably alarming. If the eye of such a one falls upon these lines—if you have persisted in saying, "Go thy way for this time; let me alone, that I may have the pleasures of this life," and have quenched the Spirit by resorting to amusements, the novel, the ballroom, or the theatre, God may have given you what you desired; but what have you now of all these pleasures? Can you look back upon them with an approving conscience? Will they bring you consolation in a dying hour? Have you not even now in your own soul, if you would make the confession, the gnawings of the worm that never dies, the burning of the fire that is never quenched? If the Spirit of God is now striving with you, it is the most momentous period of your existence. It is perhaps the turning-point between heaven and hell—the songs of angels, or the wailings of the finally lost. Beware of stifling the Spirit. Multitudes have told me the dreadful tale, "I went to scenes of amusement, or turned to the exciting romance, and I have felt no anxiety since." While the Spirit strives it is the seed-time of eternal life, the embryo of a happy immortality. Sit not down to count the loss of sinful pleasures; receive the Saviour into your heart, and you will have pleasures lasting as eternity—pleasures that leave no sting behind—pleasures that will sustain the soul when on your dying pillow, when the last trumpet shall sound, and the congregated world stand before God.

Many facts of a more cheering character might be given. The Rev. N. C——, who had a pastoral charge in M—— county, said to me, "A colporteur had left a copy of the Anxious Inquirer in the house of a wealthy man in M—— county. After some time he became interested for his salvation. One day while there on a visit I pointed him to a chapter in this book, and requested him to read it.

He read it, and soon found peace. Like every real Christian, he desired the salvation of his relations. He sent the book to his brother, a physician, who, together with a sister, were led to Christ by reading it. The book is kept in the family as an heir-loom." On another occasion Rev. Mr. C—— said he was sent for to go some distance to see a sick woman. His custom was always to carry with him a few select books to give or loan. He gave her a copy of the Anxious Inquirer, and requested her husband to read it to her. Both were irreligious; but by God's blessing on reading this book, both were led to the Saviour. A colporteur sold a copy of the same book to a man who sent it to an absent son. It led him and two of his companions to Christ. A colporteur gave a copy of Baxter's Call to a very wicked family, who never went to church. Within ten months he found the reading of it had been blessed to three of the household. A tract put into a wagoner's feed-trough while driving his team on the Sabbath, was the means of stopping him from travelling on the Sabbath, and led him to repentance. He became eminent for his piety and usefulness in the church.

A missionary who preached once a month in a wild region, and gave part of his time to colporteur work, often told me of a family that lived just beside his little mountain church, but never entered it. When he began the colporteur work he made them a visit. The man told him he did not wish him to say any thing to him on the subject of religion; that if he wanted to hear him, he could go to the church. All the time he talked and prayed, the man was muttering, and his wife increased the speed of her wheel to drown his voice. Finding all his efforts to get their attention in vain, he laid down a copy of Baxter's Call and a few tracts, and left them. On his return to fill his next appointment at the little church, to his surprise this man and his wife were in the church near the pulpit. During service they were deeply exercised. At the close he spoke to them about their souls. They told him that after he left their house they began to think about the way they had treated him, and had read his little books, and found they were great sinners. At his next communion they both joined his church, and they were among the most consistent and useful of its members.

One morning I took the stage to go to the railroad, some sixteen miles distant. There were two gentlemen in the stage. Both knew me, but I did not know them. One was a preacher, with whom I talked all the way to the dépôt. While waiting for the cars, the other passenger, a fine-looking young man, said, "I can't let this opportunity pass without making myself known to you. Do you remember laying your hand on the shoulder of a youth in the town of B—— six years ago, and urging him to seek the favor of God, and handing him a little book?" I said I had no recollection of it, as I was doing something of that sort almost every day. "Well," said he, "that talk and book were the means, I trust, of my salvation. I have since that time gone through college, and hope soon to preach the gospel." He was the son of a poor widow. He is now an able minister of the New Testament.

One day while on a journey, I came to a very small cabin on the top of a high mountain. A poor widow was by the door in very homely apparel. I asked her if she had a Bible. "No," said she, "but I have a part of a Testament, and a number of little tracts." Seeing a number of clean but poorly clad children, I began to ask them questions. The answers they gave would have done credit to most of our Sunday-school children. I asked her if she had a church or Sunday-school near. "No; there is no church or Sunday-school anywhere in reach. My children have never been in either, and I have not been at church for eight years." "Why," said I, "madam, how have you got your children so well instructed?" She ran into her cabin and brought her whole library, which consisted of a part of a Testament, and several little books and tracts sewed together, which I learned had been given her by colporteurs in their visits. Said she, "I read these to my children every Sunday, and teach them to read them, till they know all that is in them." I added to her supply little books till the countenances of herself and her children were radiant with joy, and I felt it was truly "more blessed to give than to receive."

A few miles further on I stopped at another cabin. The woman looked at me a moment. "Oh, I know you. You are the man that preached and gave us tracts at the church down on the river. I trust I was converted there. Can't you give me some tracts to give away? I am living now among very wicked people." I gave her a package, and passed on.

CHAPTER XIX.

On the invitation of several leading men, I visited L——, east of the mountains. The evening I got there the Rev. Mr. N—— called on me to "hold forth the word of life" for him that night. He stated that there was some interest in his church, and that he was unable to make any special effort, on account of his health. Although I had travelled forty miles that day by stage, in an hour I was addressing the people; and for eight days meetings were continued by exhorting and scattering tracts; at the close of which time twenty-two had professed faith in Christ, some of them among the most influential men in the city.

On the first Sabbath morning I was there, a lady of earnest piety prevailed on her husband, who was a Universalist and had been raised in that faith, and a young German whom he had employed as a clerk, to accompany her to the church. This German had been a tutor in one of the colleges in Germany, a man of fine education; but he was connected with a rebellion against the government, and had to fly in the night, and made an almost miraculous escape in disguise. He was an infidel. My subject was, "the worth of the soul;" and God truly gave me what I said. They both became awakened; and seven years after, Mr. H—— the husband of the lady joined the church, and is now an elder. He says he was never without conviction from that Sabbath morning till he yielded to Christ.

The German, Mr. S——, became intensely exercised. He attended all the inquiry meetings, and often called on the pastor, Mr. N——. His agony of mind bordered on despair. He was told again and again that whenever he could give up all for Christ he would find peace. After spending a whole night in prayer, he came to Mr. N—— in the morning, woke him out of sleep, and said, "Mr. N——, I have nothing on earth I care for but this box of rings and jewels, which my mother and sisters took from their ears and fingers the night I fled from Germany; these I have held as sacred mementos of their love. Take them, sell them, and give to the poor." Mr. N—— said, "Mr. S——, you are not far from the kingdom of God; let us pray." In a few moments he threw his arms around Mr. N——'s neck, saying, "Oh, I have found Jesus." Mr. N—— handed him back the box, and said, "Mr. S——, the Lord does not need the jewels. All he required was, that feeling of heart you manifested in giving them up." This man is now a missionary in some of the islands of the sea. His talents are all consecrated to God.

A young lady, Miss L——, very wealthy and proud, became awakened, and continued for many days on the verge of despair. She hardly ate or slept. She even became desperate: said God was not as good as his word; that she was willing to give up all for Christ, but he would not save her. We talked and prayed with her several times each day, but all in vain. At last I said to her, "Miss L——, you say you are willing to give up all for Christ?" "Yes," said she, "even life itself." "Well," said I, "in the name of my Master I ask you, out of your large wealth, to give me a donation for the Tract Society."

She replied sternly, "I am not going to buy my salvation." Said I, "The Lord can do without your money; but I have asked this to show you the deceitfulness of your own heart. You said a moment ago that you would give even life itself. Now," said I, "I shall leave you to reflect." In a few days she sent for me to rejoice with her, and the donation was heartily made

I then labored for three weeks in other churches in the city, and a large number professed religion.

Among other services, I was a week with Rev. Mr. W——, who has been for some years president of one of our auxiliary tract societies. At the close of his meeting one day, he said he would tell them what one tract had done. He gave the tract, "Have you the Wedding Garment?" to a young lady, with the request that she would go and read it over three times. She did so, and the next day she came to him as an inquirer. He then gave it to her sister, making the same request, and the next day she was an inquirer. He then gave it to a young man, and he has been led to Christ by it. "And here before you," said he, "are all three of them now rejoicing in hope."

The last month of the year 1850, I was invited by the Rev. Mr. C—— to visit M—— county, and spend a week with him at each of his charges, as he had two. The distance was ninety miles; the roads almost impassable. I shrunk from the journey; but a voice seemed to say, "You must go." When I reached the town they were holding a temperance convention, which I addressed on two occasions.

On Sunday morning I spoke first on the tract cause, and raised a collection of $150. The night service was well attended. We continued meeting twice each day, and visited families and distributed books and tracts all the rest of the time till Wednesday, but with no very marked results.

Notice had been given that meetings would begin at B——, Mr. C——'s other charge, nine miles distant, on Thursday morning at eleven. We reached there at the hour, and had only eleven hearers. At the close of the service we were invited to a Mr. B——'s to dine. He was a backslider, rich and eccentric. We had determined to visit families, talk, pray, and circulate tracts, till the time for the night service.

When we came to Mr. B——'s, the old man invited us into the parlor, and in a few minutes one of his daughters came in, a very beautiful girl, and highly educated. After a little time I introduced the subject of religion to her kindly and politely. She gave me one of the most scornful looks I ever got, and rose to leave me. I was holding in my hand the tract "*Don't be Offended;*" and just as she was passing me I presented it before her. I saw the father was offended too. Rev. Mr. C—— and I both felt unhappy; but in a few minutes we were called to dinner, and Mr. C—— introduced me to two other daughters, which made all the family.

When we were nearly through dinner, the offended one came to the table. Her eyes indicated that she had been weeping, but nothing was said. After dinner we went to another house, and met a young lady who was teacher in the female academy and also in a dancing-school. She made very light of religion, and said she preferred the ballroom to the church. I spoke to her the truth very plainly, and gave her a tract on dancing; and she turned away offended, and said she had no respect for such Puritanical religion. At night we had a tolerably good congregation, and the Lord was there indeed. Such was the state of things, that we invited all that were concerned about their souls to remain; and to our utter astonishment, the two offended ones were among them, weeping bitterly. The exhibition they had made of their wickedness had so overwhelmed them that they could scarcely wait till night to confess their sins.

The next morning we resumed our visits. The first visit was to Mr. T——'s, an elder in the church. In conversation with a daughter of his she manifested much feeling. I gave a tract to one of his sons, who, after reading it, came to his mother, and said, "Oh, mother, if I was to die as I am, my soul would be lost." That day and night the congregation was large. By this time the pious people in the church had awoke, and all were at work with books and tracts. Business was almost suspended in the village, and religion was the only theme. Almost all were inquiring the way to Zion, with the exception of half a dozen men, who threw every obstacle they could in the way. One of the worst of them went away to get out of the influence of the meetings, and was dead in three days. Another left his business and went to the country to avoid the presence of God, and has since died without hope.

The interest had become intense. On the way home from church three young ladies obtained hope almost simultaneously, and were all embraced in each other's arms. A short time after, a number of the anxious were assembled at Mr. T——'s, where I was stopping. All were pleading for mercy, but soon they began to sing praises to God. They were heard by people around, and in a short time many assembled. The new-born souls were rushing into the arms of each other, and of their fathers and mothers, and thanking them for their prayers. This joy was no doubt much like that of the day of Pentecost. One hundred and twenty-five professed their faith in Christ, and were soon after added to the churches; and so far as I have been able to learn, there was no case of backsliding. Where God does the work, the work is well done; but where it is done by mere human machinery, the results are very unsatisfactory. The town was revolutionized by this outpouring of the Spirit. The ballroom gave way to the prayer-meeting, and the drunkard's songs to those of Zion.

I gave Baxter's Call to a youth during this meeting, who told me, eight years afterwards when I met him a preacher, that that book was the means of his salvation, and had it not been for it, he never should have entered the ministry.

At another meeting some months afterwards in C——, there was a powerful work of grace, in every respect like those to which I have alluded. One old man professed faith in Christ, who was the third unbeliever in the family who had been led to Christ by the same copy of James' Anxious Inquirer.

I visited J. C. C——, a highly distinguished civilian of threescore years and ten, who had filled many important stations in life, and who now felt that his days were nearly ended. He took me by the hand very kindly, his countenance expressive of deep emotion, and said, "I am an inquirer on the subject of religion; *I have attended to every thing but my soul.*" I directed him very briefly to the Saviour, and at the close told him I would send him a little book in the morning, that would direct him more fully. He thanked me kindly for the interest I felt in him, and urged me to call again. The next morning I sent him James' Anxious Inquirer.

In four days after I called again. His health had improved. He rose to his feet, his countenance bespoke peace within, and giving me a cordial shake by the hand, he said, "I have read that little book through twice; the great question is answered. I think I understand what is meant by faith in Jesus Christ." I then explained to him as fully as I could the nature of the *new birth*—the evidences by which we might decide for ourselves the reality of the change. His very appearance was entirely changed—the deep anxiety that sat on his countenance had passed away, and happiness was expressed in every feature.

In a few days he was able to walk, and

called to see me. He said he had read the book through again; that it was "*a great book;* but the writer had omitted one important point—he did not inform the reader how long the work of sanctification must be continued after a man was justified; that justification was an act *instantaneous,* but sanctification was a work." I replied, "Our Saviour said to the thief on the cross, 'This day thou shalt be with me in paradise;' here sanctification was completed in a few hours." "I thank you, sir, that is enough: here is a check for $30, for the Tract Society; it is doing a great work."

For six years he remained steadfast in the great doctrines of salvation by faith in Christ, and in a blameless Christian life, though ever distrustful of himself. Soon after his death in February, 1856, at the age of seventy-seven, the Rev. Mr. M—— justly said of him, "Well-deserved tributes have been paid by the governor of the commonwealth, and by the legislature and other public bodies to the distinguished public worth and private virtues of this eminent citizen. His views of salvation by faith in the crucified Redeemer were clear and scriptural, and showed that the powers of a vigorous and highly cultivated mind had been brought to bear upon the all-important subject. He often expressed surprise that any one could read the holy Scriptures in the proper spirit, and not be convinced of the reality of religion, the divinity of the Saviour, and the atoning efficacy of his precious blood. His faith was simple and childlike. No dependence whatever was placed in his own merits or righteousness. The atonement of the Son of God was 'the anchor of his soul,' the basis of his hopes of heaven."

CONCLUSION.

Most of the facts and incidents in these sketches were committed to writing about the time of their occurrence, and may be relied on as simple verities. Much of deep inherent interest, which met my eye, or fell upon my ear, might have been added, but for its inappropriateness to the character of this work, or unduly swelling the narrative.

Those enjoying the calm refinements of social life in our favored cities and villages, who have never entered the abodes of ignorance and poverty in the moral wastes of the land, may be unwilling to credit even the facts related; but in a matter of such infinite importance as the enlightenment and salvation of perishing souls, could the real facts have been consistently withheld?

In the providence of God I was sent out as a watchman, not upon the walls of Zion, but *outside of those walls;* and ought I to conceal the facts, and report, "All 's well," when hundreds of thousands are dying in sin and ignorance of the great salvation? Would not such unfaithfulness be criminal in the sight of God?

And when the Holy Spirit was poured out in marvellous effusions, almost as in the day of Pentecost, should not the facts be recorded to the praise of divine grace in Jesus Christ?

Reared as I was from infancy under religious privileges, I had no idea that any part of our land was in the sad moral condition which I found actually to exist; or that the distribution of printed truth and personal labors "publicly and from house to house," were ever so richly blessed. And such erroneous and defective impressions as to the wants of our fellow-men, and the encouragements to labor for their good, I believe are very prevalent.

I remember the day when I was confident that all around me were well supplied with the Bible, but on examination I found eight families, and among them my next door neighbor, who had no Bible; and a pastor who regarded Bible efforts in his congregation as quite unnecessary, on investigation received from family after family the report,

"No Bible," the family of his own sexton being among the number. An excellent young man, now a missionary in a distant land, on faithfully exploring a wealthy county, stated what he had seen to Mr. W——, a distinguished Christian citizen. "I have heard of you," said the gentleman. "I do n't believe the statements you are making about the moral destitutions of this county. I have made up my mind to go with you and see for myself." The young man welcomed his company. In the first dwelling they entered the family had no books, not even a Bible. Said Mr. W——, "Give them $2 50 worth, and I will pay for them." In the next they entered, and in the third, they found equal destitution; and in each case Mr. W—— said, "Give them $2 50 worth, and I will foot the bill." They went further, but soon Mr. W—— said, "My young friend, the half is not told; take this $20 and go on with this heaven-directed work."

As to the rich blessing that has attended the reading of books and tracts, it is well for those reared in the midst of church privileges and good libraries to consider how different the influence of a good book may be on such as have few books, or none at all. Take, if you please, a prosperous family in the interior of the country, far from any book-store, who may have an old family Bible, a few school-books, or perhaps some other old books moral and religious. A colporteur enters with his saddle-bags of beautiful books. The children are almost frantic with joy. Each member of the family gets a book. It is devoured with greediness—not by a gospel-hardened sinner, but by one who has few or no gospel privileges.

Is it strange that such a one, on reading the Pilgrim's Progress, the Anxious Inquirer, or Come to Jesus, is immediately awakened to seek for pardon and salvation? Is it not rather *more strange*, that every one who attentively and solemnly reads such a book is not led to Christ?

And when we come down to those who are wholly destitute of books, who rarely hear a sermon, and yet are able to read, the effect is often still more powerful for good.

Notwithstanding all that has been done, I believe *one half* of all the families in our land now belong to one of these two classes.

Hence the necessity of this system of evangelization. We fear the time is far distant when our country will be so well supplied with churches and pastors as to reach the surging masses of all languages that are crowding our vast territories, seeking homes for themselves and families.

Let each one ask himself, in view of the final account he must give to God, "What can I do for these perishing thousands?" Here a way is pointed out by which every one can do something, either by *laboring*, *praying*, or *giving*. An old lady unable to move about, with an income of $600 per annum, gave $150 each year as the salary of a colporteur, and she had a few other ladies to meet her once each week to pray for God's blessing on his labors. Few men in latter days have done as much good as this colporteur, Mr. C——r. She thus labored by proxy. The man is still living who at first paid $150 for my support, and was thus instrumental in whatever good I have done. Hundreds would be ready to go and work in this department of Christian effort if means were provided.

This system of labor developes the dormant power of the church. Hundreds whose influence for good was never felt outside of their own family circle, have become successful laborers in this heaven-born work. Many of them are now able ministers of the New Testament, who would have remained "hewers of wood and drawers of water" had it not been for this system of doing good. I call to mind the names of a score of men who have been brought into the work of the ministry either directly or indirectly by this system of colportage.

Shall a work of so much power for good, and so much needed, be unsupported? The price of one ocean steamer would support it efficiently over the whole land for one year.

The issuing of this history is what the writer never intended to do, or allow others to do while he lived. He has prepared it, if he knows his own heart, purely with the hope it may do good. He trusts it may suggest to some whose supreme desire is to honor Christ in the salvation of men, a way by which they may gain the blessing of those who "turn many to righteousness," and who shall shine, above the brightness of the firmament, "as the stars for ever and ever." That this may be the gracious reward of him who writes, and of all who read this book, is the fervent prayer of THE PIONEER COLPORTEUR IN THE ALLEGHANY MOUNTAINS.

NOTE.—The labors of this single-hearted, devoted, and fearless servant of Christ were at first secured for one year to explore some of these wild mountain gorges. Having been continued five years as above, they were extended southward in the Alleghany range, and at length over the whole states of Virginia and North Carolina, till he had had the coöperation of three hundred colporteurs, and their visits had reached five hundred thousand families, over forty thousand of whom attended no place of evangelical worship. Usually they read the Scriptures, conversed, and prayed in each family; and they gathered into Sabbath-schools seventy thousand children, many of whom received their first book and learned their first lesson through this agency. Such wonderful effusions of the Holy Spirit as in some instances above recorded, were rarely witnessed, but these continued labors were evidently owned in the conversion of multitudes of souls. As the writer of the above sketches, now a commissioned minister of Christ, has well said, "It must have been the work of God, who causes weak things to confound the mighty. It was God who led the way, and raised up men and means, and guided his servants, and blessed them with his presence; and to him be all the glory."

W. A. H. SEC'Y.

NEW YORK, December, 1863.

www.ingramcontent.com/pod-product-compliance
Lightning Source LLC
LaVergne TN
LVHW010742120826
845150LV00009B/1402

* 9 7 8 1 4 2 5 5 1 7 2 6 7 *